S0-BNH-789

Introduction to American Sign Language

Introduction to American Sign Language

Harry W. Hoemann
Department of Psychology
Bowling Green State University

Illustrated by Shirley A. Hoemann

Bowling Green Press, Inc.

Bowling Green, Ohio

Copyright © Harry W. Hoemann 1986

All rights reserved. No part of this publication may be reproduced or transmitted in any form or by any means, electronic or mechanical, including photocopy, recording, or any information storage and retrieval system, without permission in writing from the author.

Library of Congress Catalog Card Number: 85-73497
ISBN: 0-9614621-0-8

Cover design by Shirley A. Hoemann

Printed in the United States of America

10 9 8 7 6 5 4

This book is dedicated to my mother:

Anna Sophie Webbink-Hoeman

Preface

This *Introduction to American Sign Language* was prepared to aid students' understanding of structural features of American Sign Language (ASL). Results obtained with draft copies of the manuscript have been very gratifying. With the help of this text and its accompanying *Workbook*, BGSU students have achieved a better grasp of ASL syntax than they had ever demonstrated previously in a one-semester course. Their accomplishments prompted the publication of these materials.

I wish to thank the many students who have assisted in the development of this text and workbook through their participation in the Sign Language Studies program at Bowling Green State University. I also wish to acknowledge the invaluable contribution of my wife, Shirley A. Hoemann, as illustrator, consultant, and publisher.

January 1, 1986

Harry W. Hoemann

Table of Contents

Introduction to American Sign Language

Chapter One: American Sign Language

A Minority Language

When laws were passed shortly after the Civil War making education compulsory, one of the underlying motives was to establish English quite firmly as the majority language so that it would be a unifying influence on the diverse cultures that were present in the United States at that time. The fact is, the United States were not very united. They had just experienced a devastating war between the states, a war that had left deep scars from Pennsylvania to Georgia. Indian uprisings were commonplace. Large numbers of immigrants were arriving from Asia and Europe with their own languages and customs. Most freed slaves were illiterate and had to be educated if they were to be assimilated into society. Compulsory education and the English language were viewed by many as the means for saving the Union by homogenizing all these diverse elements into American citizens. This country would be a melting pot, and the English language would be a very important ingredient.

The results were, at best, a partial success. The Union survived, but at the cost of many cultural traditions. Many Indian tribal languages and customs were suppressed, as were the languages spoken by many immigrants to this country. The sign language of the deaf was one of many casualties. It, too, was considered to be a foreign language, and A. G. Bell, among others, argued that there could be no excuse for teaching it in the public schools. Deaf people should be *restored to society.* They should not be encouraged to learn to use Signs, to intermarry, and to form a subculture of deaf people.

It is easier today to acknowledge that the United States is a pluralistic society and to tolerate minority languages and foreign customs. National unity is no longer threatened by the kinds of forces that were present in the late XIX Century. A rather large number of people in the United States speak some other language than English as their first language. There may be as many as 500,000 people in the United States and Canada who speak American Sign Language (ASL) as their preferred language.

Nevertheless, minority languages often stigmatize the people who use them as inferior. ASL shares this minority language stigma. In addition, since ASL makes deafness visible, it takes on the additional stigma of a handicap or disability. Students and teachers of ASL need to be honest about societal attitudes toward deafness and ASL. Consciously or unconsciously they may share some of the discriminatory attitudes toward deaf people that are a part of the majority culture's views. They need to work to improve their own and the public's awareness regarding the nature of deafness as a handicap and the status of ASL as a language.

A Visual Language

ASL is a visual language. Its symbols are visual symbols, signs made with the hands and nonmanual signs from the face and body. It is important to recognize from the outset that ASL is not, strictly speaking, a manual language. Nonmanual features of ASL are essential elements of the language. Some of these nonmanual features are grammatical features, linked to specific changes in meaning associated with their use. Others are not governed by grammatical rules, but contribute to the meaning of ASL discourse in important ways. Numerous examples of such nonmanual features will be found throughout this text Three examples will be provided here to illustrate how a nonmanual feature of ASL can systematically alter the meaning of a statement.

First, nonmanual signs mark the difference between declarative, interrogative, and imperative sentences. Declarative sentences are executed with a neutral facial expression. Nonmanual features may express the speaker's mood or state, but they would not affect the sentence type. An interrogative is executed with a questioning facial expression. In addition, the speaker is likely to maintain eye contact with the listener and to hold the final pose, awaiting an answer. There may be a forward body lean to heighten rapport. An imperative is executed with a stern facial expression, e.g., pinched lips and furrowed brows. As with an interrogative, there will be eye contact with the person to whom the command is addressed, there may be a forward body lean for rapport, and the speaker may hold the final pose awaiting a response to the command. Thus, nonmanual features are the sole means of marking the difference in ASL between declarative, interrogative, and imperative sentences.

Secondly, there are nonmanual adverbs which may be applied to a large number of verbs with similar effects on the meaning. For example, when the tongue is thrust against the inside of the teeth and lips, verbs are interpreted as done carelessly or inattentively (DRIVE-CARELESSLY, READ INATTENTIVELY). When the lips are pinched and the execution is accompanied by slightly furrowed brows, verbs are interpreted as done carefully or deliberately (DRIVE-CAREFULLY, READ-CAREFULLY).

Thirdly, there are nonmanual procedures for the speaker to communicate to the listener how the speaker feels about a particular communication. The effect is to accompany the remark with an editorial comment. For example, the ASL sentence PLANE LATE can be signed with one set of nonmanual signs to support the English translation, *I was surprised that the plane was late* and with another set of of nonmanual signs to imply *I was annoyed that the plane was late.*

Distinguishing interrogative, imperative, and declarative sentences, incorporating adverbs such as CARELESSLY or CAREFULLY, and adding editorial comments are three important roles played by nonmanual features of ASL. It is apparent that everything that can be seen on the person of the speaker is a potential source of semantic content for the listener, whether it is a manual sign or a nonmanual sign. (The terms *speaker* and *listener* will be used throughout this manual for the participants in ASL communications.) Manual and nonmanual features of ASL work in concert to generate messages that are adequate to express the speaker's intent and to satisfy the listener's informational needs, assuming that both speaker and listener are fluent in its use.

ASL does not yet have a socially useful written form. It is a visual, face-to-face language that has evolved to meet the social needs of the deaf community. One cannot write a lecture or a book in ASL. Experimental written forms of ASL have been developed for special purposes, notably by W. C. Stokoe and by Valerie Sutton. Each of these systems has certain merits. Stokoe's system has been used as a basis for a transcription system for British Sign Language at Edinburgh, and Sutton's Sign Writing appears as a regular feature of a bilingual newspaper in English and Sign Writing. The Sign Writing is set by computer. But neither Sign Writing nor Stokoe's system serve the same function in the deaf community that written English serves for the rest of society. Not enough people know them well enough to use them comfortably.

A consequence of the fact that ASL is a face to face language is that it requires good rapport between the speaker and listener. Not surprisingly, there are many devices in ASL that serve to enhance rapport, for example, the frequent use of rhetorical questions and specialized use of eye gaze. Moreover, the listener is expected to provide the speaker with constant feedback regarding the extent to which the message is understood. This all goes on unconsciously among native speakers of ASL. Students of ASL will have to make a special effort to maintain rapport with their speaker if they are the listener and with their listener(s) when they are the speaker.

National Sign Languages

Sign Language is not a universal language, although Margaret Mead, among others, has proposed that it could become one. Each country typically has its own sign language, although countries that share many cultural similarities, such as most of Canada and the United States, may share the same Sign Language. Countries that are divided along linguistic as well as cultural and political lines, such as Canada and Belgium, may have more than one sign language spoken within their borders. The Sign Language spoken by French Canadians differs considerably from the Sign Language spoken in portions of Canada where English is the dominant language. At a global level there are families of Sign Languages that share common features. Too little is known about the sign languages of the world to assign each of them to a particular family, but at least two families have been identified, namely, a far eastern family (Japan, Taiwan, China, Korea) and a western family (Europe, North America and South America).

Regional Dialects

Within a particular country there are dialect differences between different geographic regions and different racial or ethnic groups, just as there are dialect differences between spoken languages. The differences among ASL dialects are primarily differences in the lexicon and in idiomatic expressions rather than differences in grammar or syntax. In the United States, different dialects of ASL can often be traced to the usage at a residential school for the deaf, where a particular dialect may have been developed and later perpetuated among the school alumni. Thus, the dialect of Kentucky is somewhat different from the dialect of Virginia, reflecting different usages at the Kentucky School for the Deaf in Danville, KY, and the Virginia School for the Deaf in Staunton, VA. There are also differences between the dialects of ASL spoken by the black deaf community, by the Hispanic deaf community, and by the white deaf community, owing both to the degree of separation that once existed and that may still exist between black, white, and Hispanic communities and to cultural differences that persist in spite of integration in the schools. Meanwhile, there are dialect differences within the black community and within the Hispanic community, reflecting differences in educational facilities and social and cultural differences that impose boundaries on linguistic use.

Fingerspelling and the Manual Alphabet

There is a manual alphabet in ASL with which one can spell out English words (see Fig. 1). There are many fingerspelled signs in ASL that are borrowed directly from English, either as whole words, as in C-

4

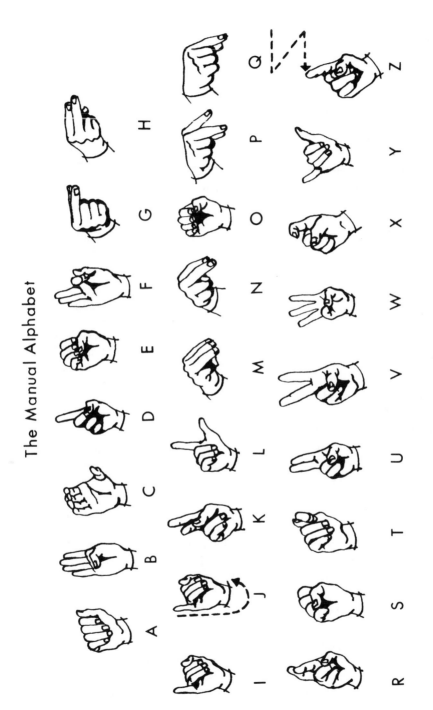

The Manual Alphabet

Fig. 1. The one-hand Manual Alphabet.

5

A-R, J-O-B, and E-A-R-L-Y, or as abbreviations, as in N-O-V, F-L-A, U-S, and T-V. However, it would be a mistake to assume that fingerspelling English is an available option for translating English to Sign. Fingerspelling is used in ASL for four very specific purposes:

(a) To refer to proper names (B-O-W-L-I-N-G G-R-E-E N).

(b) To transliterate English technical terms (S-Y-N-T-A-X).

(c) To emphasize something by spelling it out in English (B-A-D, S-A-F-E).

(d) To execute a fingerspelled sign (D-O-G, J-O-B, C-A-R).

As a translation strategy fingerspelling makes sense only when deaf people are likely to know the English word well, either as a word that they, themselves, would fingerspell, or as a word that they would use when writing English. Even then it would be useful only for a word or a phrase. To fingerspell a whole sentence, word for word, would be inappropriate.

In North America the manual alphabet is executed with one hand This alphabet is centuries old, appearing in print as long ago as 1620 in Bonet's work on the education of the deaf. The Abbe de l'Epee used a French version of this alphabet in Paris in the XVIII Century. It seems likely that this alphabet was already known in the Americas before the first school for the deaf was founded here. But when Thomas Hopkins Gallaudet brought Laurent Clerc to the United States in the early XIX Century, this virtually guaranteed that the one-handed alphabet would be the alphabet of choice in North America.

A large number of schools for the deaf were founded by people who visited de l'Epee's school in Paris and established his *French* method of teaching the deaf. They all used the one-hand alphabet. Great Britain is a major exception. Deaf people in Great Britain use a two-handed alphabet, and it is very different from the one-handed alphabet used on the Continent and in North America. Two handed alphabets are used where there has been a considerable influence from Great Britain, including Australia, India, and Indonesia. A two-handed alphabet is also used where more information needs to be represented than can be easily managed by one hand, as in Thailand. But the one-hand alphabet that was developed on the European continent and is now used in the United States is standard in most parts of the world.

It is noteworthy that even though English is spoken both in Great Britain and in the United States, ASL seems to have more in common with French Sign Language than with British Sign Language. This may reflect the strong influence that Laurent Clerc once had on deaf education and ASL usage in the United States. Laurent Clerc was trained at the Paris school by de l'Epee's successor, the Abbe Sicard. For fifty years signed English and ASL were used at the Hartford School, and Clerc was an important influence on both.

Books About Sign Languages

Books featuring descriptions or illustrations of signs have been in print for at least 150 years. An early example of such a publication is Sicard's *Theory of Signs*, (1808) which guided Thomas Hopkins Gallaudet in his early attempts to teach Alice Cogswell words and signs. Sicard's two-volume work included signs that were in use among members of the French deaf community as well as signs invented by de l'Epee to indicate features of French grammar. By means of these signs de l'Epee was able to dictate French sentences to his pupils, and they were able to write them down in French on their slate tablets. This impressed the French Academy, and the results led, eventually, to government support for the Paris school. When Sicard assumed responsibility for the school, he continued to use the *methodical signs* of de l'Epee. Clerc learned them from Sicard, and *Signed French* in Paris became *Signed English* in the United States.

In the United States early books on ASL were also descriptions of signs used by deaf people. One of the early authors of such a text was J. Schuyler Long. Religious groups also published books of signs to support religious instruction and religious services for deaf people. Books with such a religious influence were published by the Roman Catholic, Episcopal, Baptist, and Assemblies of God religious bodies. Individuals whose parents were deaf also authored books on ASL. But it was not until the 1960's that an interest in ASL led to the publication of books or monographs that were prompted by an interest in its linguistic structure.

William C. Stokoe was the pioneer in this effort. Unlike other scholars, Stokoe was convinced that ASL was a language and that its phonological structure could be studied like other languages. Since signs do not consist of sounds, the term *phonological* was not completely appropriate. But this was a minor issue. If the absence of sound made it inappropriate to refer to *phonemes* and to *phonology*, one could simply call these basic elements *cheremes*, after the Greek χειρ, or *hand*.

Stokoe's first monograph appeared in 1960. He had two main theses. The first was that signs were made up of elements or *aspects* which are presented and perceived simultaneously. They include a location, called a *tabula* or TAB, a hand configuration, called a *designator* or DEZ, and a movement, called a *signation* or SIG. Stokoe's second thesis was that the number of these elements is finite, 55 to be exact, and that they function as the basic structural features of signs. Stokoe documented his claims with evidence from contrastive analyses of signs. Sign pairs were presented in which two aspects were the same and the third

7

was different. If the change in that one aspect resulted in a change in meaning, the aspect could be said to be a distinctive feature in ASL. Examples of such sign pairs are SIT and TRAIN, where movement is the distinctive feature, THINK and ME, where location is the distinctive feature, and THINK and KNOW, where the hand configuration is the distinctive feature.

[ ] B_< ^Ωx (tab allocher, heart region)_V*like, enjoy, please;* _N *pleasure;* x *please!*

See also [ ] 5_< [♯]↓

Fig. 2. An entry from the Stokoe, Casterline, & Croneberg *Dictionary of American Sign Language on Linguistic Principles.*

Stokoe assigned symbols to the various elements that he identified, providing a means of recording ASL signs on paper (see Fig. 2). In 1965 he coauthored a dictionary of ASL with Casterline and Croneberg which is still the only genuine example of an ASL dictionary. One can look signs up in this dictionary so as to discover their meaning without having to know at the outset what they mean in English. Signs are sequenced in this dictionary in terms of the three aspects which Stokoe considered to be basic or elemental.

Other publications before and after Stokoe's have been called Sign Language dictionaries. In reality, they are Sign/English lexicons, that is, they provide English equivalents for photographs, drawings, or descriptions of signs, or they provide ASL equivalents for English words. But the term *equivalents* is a bit misleading. In many cases, the one or two English words that are listed as translating the ASL sign do not begin to do justice to its meaning. For example, the sign generally glossed NAKED can also mean an EMPTY room, a BLANK page, a VACANT house, a DESERTED town, a BARREN storeroom, *etc*. Meanwhile, the ASL equivalents for English words are equally deficient. Take the English word *hit*. One can sign HIT by making a fist and punching it into neutral space. But does this translate the word, *hit*, in *a hit movie, a pinch hit home run*, or *a hit and run victim?* Or how about the English word *fly?* What one sign would translater *fly* in *fly a plane, house fly, fly ball, fly-by-night, etc.* Ordinarily, an English word and a sign from ASL share only a portion of their respective fields of meaning. Thus, one must be very careful in using the symbol from the one language to translate the symbol from the other. Translators generally ask, first, what the symbol in the original language means. Then, they try to find a symbol in the target language that has the same or a similar meaning. It is meanings that are translated, not words or signs.

Since the ASL texts published in the United States prior to 1970 had relatively limited objectives, the books, themselves, have certain limitations. For example, minority religions have signs associated with their rituals and holiday festivals. There are signs such as RABBI, HANUK-KAH, and PASSOVER. But they are not generally found in published texts on ASL, because their authors did not have the entire scope of ASL usage in their realm of interest. Socially restricted signs, such as signs with explicit sexual connotations and signs with which one can curse or swear, were also omitted. Grammatical distinctions that were as yet unstudied when these books were compiled are not reflected in the sign descriptions, such as noun/verb distinctions (CAR vs. DRIVE) incorporated adverbs (DRIVE-CARELESSLY), reduplicated verbs (DURATIVE-WORK), *etc.* Nonmanual features are virtually ignored.

Information derived from recent ASL research is beginning to find its way into published texts on ASL. An impressive amount of research has been conducted by Ursula Bellugi and her associates at the Salk Institute in La Jolla, CA. Texts written for students and teachers of ASL now tend to include insights from this research and from research conducted in other laboratories. For example, it is now generally recognized that the signs that are described or illustrated in early texts are a kind of standard or model execution and that the sign may be modified considerably for stylistic, contextual, or grammatical reasons. The illustrated or published example of a sign is called its *citation* form. This is the form of a sign that one is likely to see demonstrated when one asks a deaf person, *What is the sign for (   )?* Students must, of course, learn the citation form of a reasonably large number of signs if they are to be able to use ASL to communicate. But they also need to be able to modify these executions so as to reflect syntactic, contextual, or stylistic constraints. They also need to be able to interpret the significance of these modifications when they occur in ASL discourse.

To aid students' vocabulary learning of citation forms of signs, the studios of WBGU-TV have produced videotapes in support of the 1000 item vocabulary texts published by the National Association of the Deaf titled *Sign Language Flash Cards* Volumes I and II. To aid students in gaining experience with the variety of executions that may occur in ASL discourse, WBGU-TV has also produced seven 30-minute programs *Deaf Models of ASL* (Nos. 1-7), featuring a variety of deaf persons engaged in casual discourse elicited by leading questions from an interviewer. Additional videotapes can be purchased or borrowed from the film library of the Merrill Learning Center at Gallaudet College in Washington, D.C. By learning to imitate the examples of ASL presented on videotapes of deaf people signing, students can learn to execute signs appropriately for a given situation or context.

One final caution is in order regarding published texts on ASL. Students need to be made aware of the fact that not all texts purporting to be texts on ASL are based on deaf usage as their model. Some of them present signs that were developed in rehabilitation settings or in educational programs to provide a code for English. Students will find signs described or illustrated in these texts that translate specific English words, such as *is, am, are, were, been, etc.* There may even be signs for English prefixes and suffixes, such as *pre-, re-, -ing, -tion, -ment, etc.* Some of these texts are appropriately titled with a specific reference to English. Others have less precise titles and may leave the impression that they are collections of signs used by deaf people. The student of ASL must have a clear notion of what it is that is to be learned, whether a code for signing English or the language used by the deaf community. This *Introduction to American Sign Language* assumes that it is the language of the deaf community that the student wishes to learn.

The Sign Space

Signs tend to be executed within a *sign space* that can be represented by a bubble surrounding the frontal region of the head and the front of the torso within easy reach without bending at the waist (see Figure 3). Signs executed within this sign space can be seen peripherally by the listener while looking at the speaker's face without breaking eye contact. Thus, the sign space is an accommodation both to the physical ability of the speaker to execute signs comfortably and to the perceptual ability of the listener to see them peripherally. Violations of this sign space carry with them specific connotations, *e.g.,* a derogatory *ieft field* execution or a satirical exaggeration of an execution.

The constraint of the sign space requires a major distinction between ASL and pantomime. Although there are elements of pantomime in ASL, they are constrained by linguistic rules. One such rule is that the mimed execution stay for the most part within the sign space that is characteristic of all ASL signs. To accomplish this, ground level is imagined to be waist high, or the palm of the nondominant hand is used to represent the ground. For example, to represent the picking of a flower, a professional mime might bend at the waist, inspect an imaginary flower on the floor, reach down and pluck it, bring it to the face with cupped hands to smell it, and then gaze off into space as if enjoying the experience. In ASL the sign FLOWER is likely to be announced at the outset as the topic of the sentence, and the sign PLUCK will be executed with hand mime or body mime. In hand mime the nondominant hand provides a frame of reference, and the plucking movement is executed on the nondominant hand's palm. In body mime the nondominant hand is unnecessary, as the dominant hand makes a plucking movement in the lower region of the sign space. The imaginary flower may be indexed by eye gaze as the sign is executed.

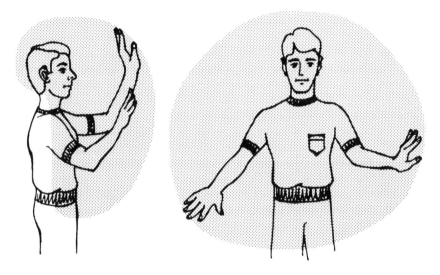

Fig. 3. The sign space consistes of a region within easy reach of the speaker and within the peripheral vision of the listener.

Speaking Styles

Languages are used in a variety of social circumstances which sometimes require a rather formal mode of speaking and which sometimes call for a very informal mode of speaking. Speakers who are at home in a language are able to switch from one speaking style to another so as to behave appropriately for the situation. Linguists call these various modes or levels of discourse *registers,* and they may enumerate specific registers that are noticeably different from one another, such as *intimate,*

informal, consultative, formal, and *frozen.* An example of a frozen register is a ritual which is always spoken in exactly the same way. An example of a formal register is a lecture or a public address. A consultative
register is used in most conversations that take place among business
associates, professionals, or acquaintances. An informal style is used
among friends and relatives. An intimate style is used among very close
friends and lovers. Needless to say, it would be highly inappropriate for
a congressman to address the House of Representatives in an intimate
style, just as it would be rather strange for a lover to speak in a formal
or frozen style. When one learns a language, one must learn how to use
the various registers of that language if one is to function appropriately
in social settings. This aspect of language learning is called *pragmatics,*
and it refers to the rules governing the appropriate social use of a
language. These rules specify who can say what to whom under what
circumstances. Students of ASL have a special problem learning the
pragmatics of ASL because they ordinarily have limited opportunities to
observe some of the registers of its use. Frozen and formal registers can
be observed by attending religious services, especially those conducted by
clergymen who, themselves, are deaf, and the business meetings of deaf
organizations, such as the National Association of the Deaf Convention.
Most classroom instruction in ASL is conducted in a consultative style of
speaking. But informal and intimate styles are more difficult to observe.
Perhaps they are also less likely to be required, especially in the early
stages of language learning. If the student of ASL finds himself or herself
frequently in social settings which require an informal or intimate style of
speaking ASL with deaf people, perhaps the deaf people who share that
setting will help the student acquire these skills.

　　Informal signing differs considerably from formal signing. In informal signing, fragment sentences are likely to occur. Socially restricted
signs may be used. Signs may be executed where the hands happen to
be, resting on a leg or a table, rather than at the location specified for
the citation form of the sign. Eye gaze is likely to be mutual for much of
the discourse, and nonmanual features are likely to carry much of the
burden of communicating. Formal signing, on the other hand, will tend
to be more carefully executed. There may be a greater reliance on signed
English. Nonmanual features will be less prominent. The signs are likely
to be executed within the sign space and in the location specified for the
citation form.

ASL and Signed English

　　It has been suggested that the distinction between ASL and Signed
English can be represented by a one-dimensional continuum and that any
manual language execution will lie somewhere along that continuum with

ASL on one end and a manual code for English at the other. This model implies that one should be able to examine a signed expression and assign it a position which would reflect the extent to which it is more ASL or more English. But there are many ways in which a manual language production can reflect an influence from English: reliance on fingerspelled English words, following English word order, inclusion of English grammatical constructions not found in ASL, or inclusion of English idioms either signed or fingerspelled. Meanwhile, a manual production can reflect influence from ASL by sequencing the signs in ways that are correct in ASL but incorrect in English, by including nonmanual features, and by using ASL idiomatic expressions. What does one do with a signed statement that has some but not all of the above examples of influences from English and some but not all of the above examples of influences from ASL? Are they all equally important, or are some more important than others? If so, what are the criteria for assigning importance to an example of one language penetrating the other? How does one put a number on these kinds of things? It seems more defensible to concede that ASL and English are not related (or opposed) to each other in such a simple fashion. A unidimensional continuum misrepresents the complexity of the ways in which these languages interpenetrate in deaf usage. If one acknowledges that ASL is a creole, having existed side by side with English in the United States for at least 150 years, influences from English are neither surprising nor compromising. They are to be expected.

For research purposes it may be necessary to make a crude judgment regarding a specific example of a manual language as to whether it contains few or many influences from English. This may be useful for evaluating the preferred mode of communication used by a particular individual or for characterizing the linguistic environment that prevails in a given setting. All too often the published reports of such research provide very little information about the linguistic abilities of the subjects or about the linguistic environments in which they are expected to function. Any attempt to characterize the linguistic experience of deaf subjects prior to the time they were tested or observed would be commendable.

Under the circumstances, what should the student of ASL strive to do? Should the student try to avoid English influences so as to construct *pure* ASL sentences? Or should the student construct simple sentences that follow English word order but use ASL signs and some nonmanual features? There is no easy answer to such questions, because a great deal depends on the purpose that the student has in mind. Teachers may wish to model examples of English sentence structure as frequently as possible for their pupils, but counselors might wish first and foremost to understand the deaf person and to be understood. Although there is

13

always considerable risk of oversimplifying, a few general comments will be offered as suggestions. First, as for *pure* ASL, it may not exist. Creoles always show some influence from the other language in the mix. Moreover, if the student's goal is to be able to communicate with deaf people rather than to master the details of ASL grammar and syntax, trying to purge one's manual language productions of all traces of English may be more trouble than it is worth. Deaf people generally have considerable experience communicating with hearing people whose ASL skills are limited. They may even accommodate to the linguistic competence of their listener and sign English. It seems likely that communication between deaf and hearing people will always be affected by the unequal competence that they tend to have in each other's preferred language.

When hearing people sign to deaf people relying on English to provide most of the grammatical structure, the result is a pidgin. It is called Pidgin Sign English (P.S.E.). Ordinarily, a pidgin has only temporary utility. It is not learned by children from their parents. It is not generally taught in school. If the foreman on a construction site speaks one language and the workers speak another, they will concoct a mode of communicating that borrows from both languages and reflects a simplified grammatical structure. Once the building is completed and the parties go their separate ways, the pidgin they have invented will be forgotten. But P.S.E. is not an ordinary pidgin. It is used by too many people in too many circumstances to be quickly forgotten. Moreover, it has become quite powerful as a mode of communication, serving as the medium for public education, for interpreting at conferences and symposia, and for some televised productions featuring Sign. P.S.E. is now sometimes taught in school in programs where the administration has implemented a program requiring teachers to sign English to their pupils.

It is not wrong for students of ASL to make use of P.S.E. to communicate with deaf people. But it is important that they understand the difference between ASL and P.S.E. ASL is a language. P.S.E. is a compromise between two languages, ASL and English.

Summary

American Sign Language is a creole, with a unique grammar and syntax but reflecting many influences from English. It is spoken by up to 500,000 people in the United States and Canada. For a long time ASL was disparaged as an inferior language, lacking in grammatical structure and confining deaf people to a subculture of users. Since it makes deafness visible, there is a stigma attached to ASL derived from its association with a disability. More recently linguists have demonstrated that ASL is a language in the full sense of the term, and many educators and behavioral scientists have begun to champion the rights of deaf people to use ASL as their first or native language.

ASL has some unique features. Since it is a visual language, it involves close rapport between the speaker and listener. It also includes many nonmanual features, such as facial expressions and body language, in addition to manual signs.

Contrary to public opinion, Sign Language is not a universal language. Occasionally two countries share the same sign language, *e.g.*, Canada and the United States. But generally each country has its own sign language, and some countries have more than one major sign language spoken within their borders. Dialect differences also exist, reflecting divisions among racial or ethnic minorities and a particular geographic region whose boundaries are often associated with one or another residential school for the deaf.

A manual alphabet makes it possible to fingerspell English words. This is a common strategy for representing proper names. It is also used for technical terms or for emphasis. Some words are spelled so frequently that they become fingerspelled signs.

Books about Sign Languages have been around for a long time, but only recently have they begun to reflect the results of linguistic research on the structure of sign languages. Pioneering work on the structure of ASL was carried out by W. C. Stokoe in the 1960's. More recently Ursula Bellugi at the Salk Institute and researchers in other laboratories have contributed a great deal to our knowledge about ASL grammar and its strategies for communicating meanings.

Different social situations call for different styles of speaking, ranging from intimate or informal to formal or even frozen styles. Students of ASL need to learn to adjust their style of speaking to fit the circumstances. Pragmatics is the branch of linguistics that deals with the rules governing the appropriate social use of a language.

It is important to distinguish between ASL, the language spoken by the deaf community, and Pidgin Sign English, which is a means by which deaf and hearing people often communicate with each other. A pidgin is a convenient device for communicating among people who are not equally fluent in each other's language. Ordinarily a pidgin has only a limited utility and a short history, but Pidgin Sign English is a relatively powerful system, and it is used in many settings where deaf and hearing persons need to communicate.

[handwritten notes: lab - location; sig - hand sign; - movement; direction of palms also important]

Chapter Two: Sentences in American Sign Language

What is a sentence?

Humans use languages to express thoughts. To accomplish this, they construct sentences. One could debate at length over a proper definition for a sentence. Rather than indulge in such an endless discussion, we shall assume that a sentence in a spoken language is a group of words which expresses a complete thought. In sign languages we shall also assume that a sentence expresses a complete thought, but with two important differences. Signs are used instead of words, and nonmanual features play an important grammatical role. Even in spoken languages the tone of voice and the body language of the speaker can contribute to the meaning of a sentence. But these are generally considered to be paralinguistic features of spoken languages, unessential for the central meaning of a sentence. A written sentence, for example, is considered to be capable of expressing a complete thought without additional clues from the tone of voice or facial expression of a speaker. Sign languages are different. Nonmanual features are part and parcel of the language. Thus, we must define a sentence in a sign language as a group of manual and nonmanual features which expresses a complete thought.

Since this is the case, a word of caution is in order regarding the use of glosses to represent ASL sentences. Glosses are representations of ASL sentences that specify the sequence in which a string of signs is executed, e.g., THINK ME RAIN MAYBE STOP. They are useful for providing some information regarding some characteristics of an ASL sentence or a string of signs. But a great deal of information is not included. Some manual features are lost, including changes in the size of the execution or changes in the rhythm or tempo of the execution. Nonmanual features are also lost, including spatial organization and facial and body cues.

To compensate for these losses of information, researchers have developed elaborate coding systems for representing nonmanual features of ASL on paper along with information regarding the specific sign that was used and the sequence with which a string of signs was executed. The time that it takes for each component of a sentence to be executed is also often represented graphically. For data on ASL syntax such transcripts are absolutely necessary. For instructional purposes a detailed transcript is generally not required, and glosses can serve a useful function. But students of ASL must be aware that a gloss represents only the sequence of a string of signs, not the entire set of signals from which a listener might derive their meaning.

Manual Features of ASL

Manual features of ASL include the following:

(a) A lexicon of *Signs* executed with one or both hands.

(b) Handshapes which serve as *Size and Shape Specifiers* (a special kind of adjective).

(c) Handshapes which serve as *Classifiers* (representing the location or the movement of one or more nouns).

(d) Handshapes that serve as an *Index* (referring to a location or to a noun associated with that location).

(e) Handshapes for letters of the *Alphabet* and for *Numerals*.

(f) *Graphic depiction,* which serves an adjectival function.

(g) *Sign mime,* which serves a verbal function.

The manual features of ASL can be modified in accordance with grammatical rules so as to change the meaning of signs or groups of signs in a sentence. Subtle changes in the rhythm and tempo of signing, reduplicating (repeating) signs two or more times, sometimes with a characteristic movement, signing with more or less force or vigor, or changing the size or location of an execution can affect the meaning of signs and of sentences in rule-governed ways. Adverbs of manner are often incorporated in the execution of verbs, and adjectives can sometimes be incorporated in the manner of executing nouns. Sentences in ASL do not consist of signs which stand one-to-one in place of words. ASL sentences are composed of features not found in English, and many things that are expressed in English by means of words are expressed in ASL by other means, such as modifications in the execution of signs or by nonmanual features.

Nonmanual Features of ASL

Nonmanual features of ASL include the following:

(a) Several aspects of *facial expression*, including brows, lips, tongue, eyes, and facial muscles.

(b) Several aspects of *body language,* including orientation, muscle tone, body lean, and loose or hunched shoulders.

(c) *Spatial organization* of the information that is to be included in a sentence or narrative and the execution of signs so as to agree with this spatial organization.

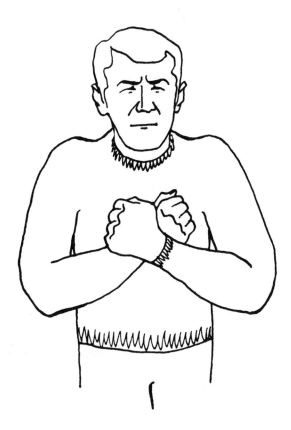

Fig. 4 Pursed lips and furrowed brows may imply intensity rather than hostility.

Nonmanual features of ASL are not merely natural gestures or a universal body language. They are governed by linguistic rules. For example, the facial expressions that mark a verb as an action done carelessly, intensely, continually, repeatedly, *etc.* are generalizable to a large number of verbs, and they always mean the same thing. Specific nonmanual features may be misunderstood by someone not familiar with the language. For example, pinched lips and furrowed brows may imply anger or hostility to the uninitiated observer. But in ASL this facial expression may serve to intensify a verb or an adjective (see Figure 4). Such an intense facial expression may accompany the verb, LOVE, in MY MOTHER LOVE APPLE PIE or the adjective WONDERFUL in MY VACATION LAST-YEAR WONDERFUL.

The importance of nonmanual features of ASL is especially apparent in the distinction between declarative, interrogative, and imperative sentences, discussed below. The nonmanual features are the only distinguishing features of these sentences. The sentence YOU STOP can mean *You stopped, Did you stop?* or *Stop!* depending on the accompanying nonmanual features. A nonmanual negation, a headshake, is also common in ASL. A negative headshake may accompany a verb or an entire sentence to negate the statement. For example, the sentence ME SEE MOVIE accompanied by a negative headshake would be translated, *I did not see the movie.* The manual features taken alone would be construed as the exact opposite.

Subject/Predicate Sentences

Like English, ASL has sentences composed of a subject and a predicate. A subject may be a noun, a pronoun, a noun phrase, or a noun clause. A predicate may be a verb or a verb and its complement. An example of a Subject/Predicate sentence is WIND CHANGE.

Topic/Comment Sentences

Sentences in ASL may also be constructed as a topic followed by one or more comments. An example of a Topic/Comment sentence is MY CAR: INDEX-IT OLD INDEX-IT. The topic in Topic/Comment sentences must be marked for the listener by means of nonverbal cues. Typically, the speaker will establish mutual eye gaze before announcing the topic. The eye gaze may be sustained while the topic is defined, and the speaker may await some response from the listener that the topic has been understood. This is an example of the special rapport that characterizes ASL. A questioning facial expression or a nod of the head may accompany the establishment of the topic. Once the listener has acknowledged that the topic is understood, the facial expression is likely to change for the comment. Topic/Comment sentences should be translated into English as Subject/Predicate sentences.

Since the topic of a Topic/Comment sentence corresponds to the subject of a Subject/Predicate sentence, Topic/Comment sentences can be constructed in English. One can say *As for my car, it is old*. But this is an unusual way of speaking. In ASL Topic/Comment sentences are not unusual. They appear to be especially appropriate in a visual language. One needs to know what one is talking about before one can assimilate what is being said about it.

Once a topic is established in ASL, it can be referenced with an index. The index may precede the comment or follow the comment or both. Examples of such Topic/Comment sentences with an index before and after the comment are as follows:

FARMER: INDEX-THEY NEED RAIN INDEX-THEY.

DAUGHTER: INDEX-SHE LIVE CALIFORNIA INDEX-SHE.

MOUNTAINS: INDEX-THEY BEAUTIFUL INDEX-THEY.

CITY: INDEX-IT BIG INDEX-IT.

An index may bracket the predicate in other topic comment sentences even when the topic would be the object of a Subject/Predicate sentence, and the index refers to the subject. Examples follow:

MONEY: ME HAVE NONE ME.

SMOKE: ME QUIT ME.

SNOW: ME DON'T-WANT ME.

Declarative, Interrogative, and Imperative Sentences

Both Subject/Predicate and Topic/Comment sentences can be either declarative, interrogative, or imperative sentences. A declarative sentence states a fact. WIND CHANGE. An interrogative sentence asks a question. WIND CHANGE? An imperative sentence expresses a command (to the wind in this case). WIND, CHANGE! The difference between declarative, interrogative, and imperative sentences in ASL is marked nonmanually (Figure 5).

A declarative sentence is typically executed with a neutral facial expression. If a special facial expression colors the meaning, it is some other semantic aspect of the sentence, not the basic sentence type that it defines.

An interrogative sentence is marked by several nonmanual features, which may occur in different combinations. The full battery of nonmanual features that may accompany an interrogative are

  (a) A questioning facial expression, *e.g.*, arched eyebrows and wrinkled forehead.

Fig. 5. Nonmanual cues mark the difference between interrogatives (FINISH?) and imperatives (FINISH!).

(b)   A forward lean of the body.

(c)   A sustained mutual eye gaze with the listener.

(d)   A hold of the final pose.

The brief final hold is apparent even when the question is a rhetorical question, namely, one to which an answer is not expected. The sustained eye gaze may reflect the speaker's expectation that the listener will respond to the question. The forward body lean reflects the heightened rapport that characterizes a discourse during a question.

The carrier phrase, DO-YOU often introduces a question. This is true in English as well as in ASL. However, in ASL a special consideration arises, since the fingerspelled DO-YOU resembles the tracing of a question mark. When it occurs at the end of a sentence, the resemblance to a question mark is especially striking. The following sentences are glossed with DO-YOU at the beginning and end of each sentence. (In actual usage, it is optional whether DO-YOU occurs in both places.)

DO-YOU LIKE COFFEE DO-YOU?

DO-YOU NEED C-A-R DO-YOU?

DO-YOU HAVE ENOUGH MONEY DO-YOU?

An imperative sentence issues a command. Imperative sentences are marked by the following nonmanual features:

(a) Furrowed brows.

(b) A forward body lean.

(c) A sustained eye gaze with the listener to whom the command is given.

As in the case of a question, the forward body lean and the sustained eye gaze may reflect the rapport that is in place during a command. The speaker expects the listener to pay attention and to respond to the command. Furrowed brows signal the intensity associated with an imperative.

In English the subject of an imperative sentence is usually understood. It may occur, as in *You, go home.* But it is not required. *Go home,* is sufficient. In ASL the subject is also not likely to be represented by a sign, YOU, but there is an additional requirement not present in English. In ASL, the speaker is likely to establish mutual eye gaze with the person to whom the command is to be given. The only exception to this rule is when an imperative verb is signed directionally at the person who is expected to respond to the command. Thus, FINISH, for *Stop that,* may be signed behind the teacher's back at an unruly class without the teacher having to turn around and establish eye contact. But this is the exception. Ordinarily the speaker will make sure that the listener's attention is assured by mutual eye gaze before the command is issued.

Simple, Compound, and Complex Sentences

Two elements are essential for a sentence, namely, a substantive as a subject and a verb as predicate. By combining these elements with modifiers and complements, sentences of varying length and complexity can be constructed. As a matter of fact, the only limits on the length and complexity of a sentence are the speaker's ingenuity and the listener's ability to interpret the result.

A simple sentence consists of a single subject and a single predicate. The example given previously is WIND CHANGE. A longer sentence that is also a simple sentence is MY MOTHER VISIT ME IN CALIFOR-NIA. The second sentence includes modifiers, the possessive pronoun MY, the object, ME, and the prepositional phrase, IN CALIFORNIA. The complete subject is MY MOTHER, and the complete predicate is VISIT ME IN CALIFORNIA.

A simple sentence can have a compound subject. An example is
MY MOTHER SISTER VISIT ME IN CALIFORNIA. It would be permissible to sign MY MOTHER AND MY SISTER, but the conjunction
AND is usually communicated through nonmanual features, such as a
brief juncture marker, and by the rhythm and tempo of the execution of
the sentence. In the present case, both MOTHER and SISTER might be
executed with a slight forward movement of the shoulders, a movement
that would be identical for both signs. The compound subject MOTHER
and SISTER are both joined to the same predicate, VISIT ME IN CALI-
FORNIA.

A simple sentence can have a compound predicate. MY FRIEND
LIVE WORK IN NEW-YORK. As before, the conjunction, AND, is
optional and omitted. The complete predicate includes the prepositional
phrase, IN NEW-YORK, which modifies both verbs. Compound predi-
cates are common in ASL, because speakers often follow narrative order,
stringing verbs together in a long sequence. An example of such a narrative string is ME GO, LOOK, THINK, DECIDE. There are four verbs in
this sentence, GO, LOOK, THINK, and DECIDE.

One should not assume that a simple sentence is not complexly constructed. The term *simple* refers only to the type of sentence structure
that is being used. A simple sentence can have a compound subject and
a compound predicate and still be a simple sentence.

Compound sentences are formed by linking one simple sentence to
another. In English this is usually done with a conjunction, such as *and*
or *but*. In ASL these conjunctions are used only when special emphasis is
required. In most cases the link between adjacent simple sentences is
established by means of the rhythm and tempo of the execution and by
means of nonmanual features. An example of a compound sentence
without a specific sign for a conjunction is ALL DRY, ALL WITHER. A
brief pause would separate the two clauses, and a terminal juncture
would mark the end of the statement. The same facial expression could
be sustained for the entire statement. An example of a compound sentence in which a conjunction might be used is TEMPERATURE DROP
BUT SNOW? NO. In this case there would also be a brief pause after
DROP, but there would also be a change of facial expression, indicating
that the second clause represents a change in mood or intent. Other
examples of compound sentences follow:

SKY BLUE AND SUNSHINE WARM

WIND CHANGE AND TEMPERATURE DROP

RAIN STOP AND SNOW BEGIN

ME THERE NEVER BUT AREA WHERE? ME KNOW

TEACHER STRICT BUT DAUGHTER STILL LIKE

Complex sentences are constructed of at least one main clause and at least one subordinate clause. These are sometimes called an independent clause and a dependent clause. Both the main clause and the subordinate clause will have a subject and a predicate. The subordinate clause can be a causal clause, a conditional clause, a relative clause, or a substantive clause.

A causal clause can be introduced by the sign BECAUSE. ME VISIT DOCTOR BECAUSE ME SICK. Causal clauses can be avoided, and they often are, by inserting a rhetorical WHY? after the main clause and then answering the question. ME VISIT DOCTOR. WHY? ME SICK. The English translation would probably retain the causal clause: *I visited the doctor because I was sick.*

A conditional clause may be introduced by the sign IF. This is sometimes executed as a fingerspelled sign, I-F. An example is IF TEMPERATURE DROP, WILL BEGIN SNOW. Alternatively, the condition can be posed as a question: HAPPEN TEMPERATURE DROP? WILL BEGIN SNOW. Even when IF or I-F are used to introduce a conditional, a questioning facial expression is still appropriate as the condition is being stated.

A relative clause is introduced by a relative pronoun or a relative adverb. Examples of relative pronouns in English are *who, whose, which, that, etc.* Examples of relative adverbs in English are *how, why, where, since, after, before, as, etc.* Both relative pronouns and relative adverbs are found in ASL. An example of a relative clause introduced by a relative pronoun is PEOPLE THEY LIVE CITY BIG THEY MUST COMMUTE FAR. This sentence would be translated into English: *People who live in a big city must commute far.* An example of a relative clause introduced by a relative adverb is WHEN ME GET NEW C-A-R, ME WILL DRIVE CALIFORNIA. Relative clauses are found in ASL. But a visual language does not lend itself well to a great many embedded constructions. The nursery rhyme, *The House that Jack Built,* would not fare well in ASL translation. Relative clauses, like causal clauses, are often avoided. When a speaker in English uses a great many complex sentences in an address that is to be interpreted for a deaf audience, interpreters often have a difficult time making the meaning clear. Speakers should be advised when composing a speech that is to be translated that there are rules for writing translatable prose. One of them is to avoid complex sentences.

Substantive clauses take the place of nouns. They may become the subject of a verb (THAT WE GET VACATION MAKE ME HAPPY) or the object of a verb (THINK ME RAIN MAYBE STOP). In English these sentences tend to introduce the substantive clause with, *that.* In

25

ASL THAT is unnecessary. Complex sentences constructed of substantive clauses as objects of a verb are quite common in sentences with the verbs THINK, WISH, FEEL, DREAM, DECIDE, *etc.*

ASL and English Sentence Structure

Students should be cautioned not to take the structure of an English sentence which happens to express their intended meaning as a guide to constructing an ASL sentence that is to mean the same thing. English tends to use a great many complex sentences as the preferred means for embedding information in a single statement. ASL is also capable of coding complex information, but it tends to do it by other means than by constructing sentences with one or more dependent clauses. In any case, when constructing ASL sentences, one should be coding meaning directly into ASL, not translating or transliterating English words. To illustrate this point, three English sentences will be cited which are fully translatable into ASL but not by means of a similar surface structure.

(a)   It was raining very hard against the window that I was looking out of.

(b)   I couldn't believe it, but my friend kept changing his mind about buying a new car.

(c)   When I was in school I wished that I had finished and had a job, but now that I am working, I wish that I were back in school

The first of these sentences requires only three signs, ME WINDOW RAIN. All of the additional information is communicated by the manner in which these signs are executed or by nonmanual features of the execution. First, the sign ME is topicalized, to mark it as a topic for the sentence. Second, WINDOW, is also named as a topic, but it is executed very near the face, with the eyes peering through the opening formed by the two hands as the sign is executed. Finally, the sign RAIN is executed directionally, at an angle toward the face of the speaker and toward the imaginary window that the signer is looking out of. The execution of RAIN is intense, with a repeated, forceful execution, driving the sign downward toward the window and the speaker's face. The muscles of the face are tensed, the eyes are squinted half shut, the face is turned slightly away from the window as if to avoid the impact of the rain, but not enough to break the eye gaze through the imaginary panes. If one were to start with the English original and attempt a translation, it is unlikely that the proposed ASL version would be the result. Of course, there are many correct translations of any original. But the proposed ASL version is faithful to the meaning of the original, and it accomplishes its task by combining manual and nonmanual features in a reenactment of the experience, sharing with the listener not only what took place but also how the speaker felt about it.

The second sentence, *I couldn't believe it, but my friend kept changing his mind about buying a new car,* requires that the friend's intent be established first. We can topicalize MY FRIEND and then index the topic so as to add the comment. MY FRIEND: HE WANT BUY NEW C-A-R HE. The next statement can convey the information that he kept changing his mind. Fortunately, ASL has an inflection that implies an iterative event, one that is repeated over and over in relatively quick succession. Moreover, the verb, CHANGE, lends itself well to the notion that the repeated action was a series of reversals, first one way and then the other. The normal execution of the verb CHANGE is in a left to right rotation of the dominant right hand as the opposed left hand exchanges places with the right. Once this execution is completed, one can execute the same sign again in reverse to indicate that the original CHANGE has been undone, and conditions are reversed. This same execution of CHANGE can be applied to the weather, to the stock market, or to any other topic subject to change. In this case, we can sign HE MIND CHANGE, CHANGE, CHANGE, CHANGE. Meanwhile, we wish to convey the impression that the speaker was taken aback by his friends indecision. One way to do this is to portray with the facial expression the surprise of the speaker at the same time that the verb CHANGE is being executed. Alternatively, the speaker could add at the end, ME CAN'T BELIEVE. It is likely that both the nonmanual and the manual expression would be used. The complete translation, then, of the second sentence, is MY FRIEND: HE WANT BUY NEW C-A-R HE. HE MIND CHANGE, CHANGE, CHANGE, CHANGE (accompanied by a facial expression indicating growing amazement). ME CAN'T BELIEVE.

There is an alternative sign that could be used for CHANGE-MIND. It is executed with the "V" hand at the forehead with contact made first with the tip of the middle finger and then with the tip of the index finger. To represent repeated changes of the mind, the action, may be reversed and then reversed again, yielding HE MIND-CHANGE, MIND-CHANGE, MIND-CHANGE.

The third sentence is an example of a compound sentence in which each of the component sentences is complex. Each of them has a substantive clause as the object of the verb, *wish,* and both of them have a subordinate clause introduced by a relative adverb, *when* or *now that.* The entire sentence reads, *When I was in school, I wished that I had finished and had a job, but now that I am working, I wish that I were back in school.* We need a past tense marker for this sentence to establish the fact that the first sentence of the two compound sentences took place in the past. AGO will serve as such a marker. AGO ME IN SCHOOL, ME

27

WISH FINISH, WISH HAVE J-O-B. A juncture marker would separate the three clauses. Notice the redundant WISH, which helps to organize the information in the first of the two main clauses. For the second main clause a change in tense is needed as we shift from the past to the present. NOW is the appropriate temporal adverb for this purpose. NOW ME WORK. Again we can rely on redundancy to provide structure for the statement. NOW ME WORK, NOW ME WISH STILL SCHOOL. Brief pauses would mark the junctures after WORK and WISH.

Fragment Sentences

Not all ASL sentences are well formed. Sentence fragments occur, not only in informal conversation, but also in formal discourse. Sometimes the speaker recognizes a slip of the tongue (or hand) and retracts the statement, rephrasing the message. Other times the speaker is unaware of the mistake, and the listener will have to recognize the intended meaning.

Fortunately, ASL is sufficiently redundant that the meaning is generally preserved even under adverse conditions. One could probably eliminate every fifth sign from a narrative and still have most of the meaning come through. One can sign with only one hand when the other hand is encumbered (with a baby, a grocery bag, or a drink), and there does not seem to be any loss of meaning at all.

Sometimes a sentence that appears to be ambiguous to an observer may be well understood by close friends or relatives, who share with the speaker many memories of prior experiences. Mutual knowledge of facts makes it unnecessary to spell them out.

Students should not be encouraged to construct fragment sentences or ungrammatical sentences on purpose, but they may wish to learn how to signal the listener that they want to retract a statement.

Juncture Markers

Examples of ASL sentences cited previously have included mention of juncture markers. These are dividers that separate phrases and clauses from each other. They are what make it possible to decide which signs belong together and which do not. Signs which lie on opposite sides of a juncture marker probably do not belong to the same phrase or clause, whereas signs which are clustered together with a juncture marker on either side should probably be interpreted as part of the same grammatical construction. Pauses, changes in facial expression, shifts of eye gaze, or changes in body orientation may function as juncture markers in ASL. Within a sentence, slight pauses, body shifts, or changes in facial expression or eye gaze mark boundaries between phrases or dependent

clauses. Longer pauses or more pronounced nonmanual cues mark junctures between sentences. When there is a complete change of topic or a
digression to a previous subject under discussion, a sign may announce
the juncture. Examples of such signs are MOVE-DOWN, PUT-ASIDE,
REFER-BACK, *etc.* These signs tend not to be included in published
lists, because they do not have real-world referents. Several of them
have been included in *Sign Language Flash Cards* Vol. II. They are
rather important for providing some of the mechanics of communicating,
especially in a formal register.

Discourse Processes

Discourse involves the rules for carrying on a conversation with one
or more people in a social situation. It involves procedures for gaining
someone's attention, for initiating or terminating a discourse, for inter-
rupting and for avoiding interruption, for ascertaining whether the
listener is comprehending the speaker's messages and, in the case of the
listener, for signaling whether the message is or is not understood.

Eye gaze plays a particularly important role in turn taking during
ASL conversations. A sustained eye gaze after the completion of a statement is a clear signal that the speaker is yielding the floor to the listener
and expects the listener to begin speaking. On the other hand, if the
speaker averts the eye gaze, avoiding eye contact with the listener, this
effectively prevents the listener from gaining the attention of the speaker
so as to interrupt or seize the floor. Meanwhile, listeners can cut a
speaker off by looking away. Children of deaf parents quickly learn that
they can *silence* their parents by looking away from them. Parents learn
equally quickly to grasp the child's head firmly so as to force mutual eye
contact. One can occasionally observe parent-child interactions in which
the parent has the child's head in a firm grasp about three inches from
their own, and the child is trying desperately to look off to the side so as
to avoid "hearing" what the parent has to say. The parent usually wins
these contests.

Hearing people need to be especially careful about their use of eye
gaze, since they may not realize how much significance it may have in an
ASL conversation. For example, hearing people may have been cultur-
ally conditioned to avert eye gaze occasionally rather than gaze directly
at the speaker for an extended period of time. Such a direct eye gaze
may become uncomfortable for a hearing person to sustain, especially
when the other person is a member of the opposite sex or a person of
high status. To satisfy the trained compulsion not to be too forthright or
direct, the hearing person may break eye gaze. But this break in eye
contact may be interpreted by the deaf person as a signal that the hearing person is no longer interested in paying further attention to the

conversation. What began as a rule to be polite and not stare at people becomes a rude insult, tantamount to rejection. The hearing person may not have intended to signal a rejection, but that is how deaf people are likely to interpret a break in eye gaze initiated by the listener.

Many of the rules for discourse are included in pragmatics, the branch of linguistics that examines the appropriate use of language in social settings. Very little has been written about the pragmatics of ASL, and much of what has been written has been based on the personal experiences of the authors. Anecdotal evidence is not a good substitute for scientific data. Unfortunately, the data are in short supply. The student of ASL will find no clear guidelines to avoiding social blunders in the use of ASL within the deaf community. Even among friends and with full knowledge of the language that is spoken, it is easy to be rude, insensitive, or thoughtless of other people. It is 100 times easier to make social blunders in a strange culture and with a strange language. Fortunately (or unfortunately, depending on one's point of view), deaf people have had considerable experience with the social blunders of hearing people. Most of them are patient and forgiving, recognizing that there are many things about deafness and communicating with deaf people that hearing people simply do not understand. Meanwhile, by means of careful observation, the student can learn to appreciate the many strategies that are available to the deaf linguistic community as it uses ASL as its communicative channel and the subtle nuances of meaning that can be conveyed by its manual and nonmanual features.

SUMMARY

Sentences in ASL may take the form of a Subject/Predicate construction or a Topic/Comment construction. Subject/Predicate sentences may be simple sentences, with one subject and one predicate, or the may be compound sentences, in which two simple sentences are joined together. Subject/Predicate sentences may also be complex sentences, which consist of one or more main clauses and one or more subordinate clauses. The subordinate clauses of a complex sentence can be causal clauses, conditional clauses, relative clauses, or substantive clauses. Simple and compound sentences are more common in ASL than complex sentences. The complexity that English and other spoken languages achieve by means of embedded clauses is often achieved in ASL by other means.

Topic/Comment sentences mark a topic nonmanually and, then, make a comment that pertains to the topic. The subject of a subject/predicate sentence corresponds to the topic of a topic/comment sentence.

A sentence in ASL consists of both manual and nonmanual features. The manual features, signs and handshapes, convey semantic content both through the meaning of the sign or the handshape and through the relationship between these elements within a sentence. Nonmanual features often add important semantic content, such as whether the sentence is declarative, interrogative, or imperative, whether the sentence is affirmative or negative, and how the speaker feels about the semantic content of the message.

Juncture markers place boundaries around the phrases and clauses within a sentence, providing information as to which signs within a sentence are to be interpreted as belonging together. Examples of juncture markers are pauses, changes in facial expression, changes in eye gaze, shifts in body orientation, and explicit signs, such as MOVE-ON, PUT-ASIDE, REFER-BACK, *etc.*

Eye gaze plays an especially important role in ASL discourse, since it governs turn taking in ASL conversations. If a speaker does not wish to be interrupted, the speaker will simply avoid making eye contact with the listener. If a listener wants to cut a speaker off, the listener can break eye contact and look away. When a speaker establishes eye contact with the listener and pauses, this is a clear signal that the speaker is yielding the floor to the listener and expects the listener to become the speaker.

The branch of linguistics that covers the rules of conversation and discourse is pragmatics. The student of ASL will find very little information on the pragmatics of ASL in print. The best source of information is the deaf community, and the best access to that source is careful observation.

Chapter Three: Nouns in American Sign Language

Nouns as a Part of Speech

A noun is the name of a person, place, or thing. There are common nouns (HOUSE) and proper nouns (NEW-YORK). There are count nouns (TREE) and mass nouns (WATER). Nouns are singular (MAN) and plural (MEN); they are masculine (FATHER), feminine (MOTHER), or neuter (BOOK). Nouns may serve as the subject of a sentence as in *CAR* OLD, or the object of a verb, as in HE SELL *CAR*. Nouns may be indirect objects, as in ME GIVE *SISTER* BOOK, objects of prepositions, as in ME WORK IN *FACTORY*, and objects of infinitives, as in ME WANT BUY *CAR*. Nouns can even be used as adjectives, as in *BABY* BUGGY, *BABY* DOLL, *FARM* LIFE, and *CITY* LIFE. If nouns can be and do all of these things, languages must have a set of strategies for marking nouns as to number, gender, case, and even as nouns and not verbs. ASL is no exception.

Derivation of Nouns

Nouns in ASL are derived from a wide variety of sources. At a rather iconic level, signs may imitate a global representation of the thing symbolized (BOOK, HOUSE, RAIN, BOAT). These signs resemble a graphic depiction. Other signs may focus on only one aspect of the referent, a distinctive feature of the thing symbolized (a cow's horn, a clown's nose, or a policeman's badge).

Nouns may also be derived from mime. Some of these nouns are derived from a characteristic action performed by the thing symbolized (FISH, POPCORN, DOOR), and some are derived from the action performed by someone using the thing symbolized (TEA, GOLF, ICE-CREAM).

A handshape may represent an object, sometimes as a one handed sign (AIRPLANE, TELEPHONE) and sometimes with the nondominant hand serving as a base (GLASS, CUP). Parts of the body can be referenced by touching them (NOSE, EAR) or by pointing to them (FEET).

A sizable percentage of signs in ASL are sufficiently iconic that even persons with no prior knowledge of the language can guess their meaning. These are called *transparent*. Still others are plausible in retrospect (COLLEGE, RABBI, WAR). These are called *translucent*. The percentage of iconic signs in ASL is not high enough for naive observers to guess the meaning of sentences. As a matter of fact, an equally high percentage of signs tend to produce guesses that are similar but wrong. The signs COUNT, CALL, TRUE, GOVERNMENT, and EXCEPT have been thought to mean *climb, slap, quiet, think* and *pick up*, respectively.

The iconicity of a sign does not reside in the sign itself. It comes from a *perceived* relationship between the sign and its referent. For this reason it will differ from one culture to another and, within each culture, from one individual to another on account of age or experience. The sign HOUSE is iconic only to a society where houses are built with pitched roofs; the sign COLLEGE is iconic only to people who know the sign SCHOOL; and the sign SHEEP is iconic only to people who know that sheep are sheared for their wool.

At a time when ASL was considered to be something less than a language, its iconicity was cited as a deficiency. Now that the status of ASL is no longer in doubt among responsible linguists, its iconicity is no longer a central issue.

There has been a historical trend away from iconicity. Signs that were once highly iconic are now more arbitrary, and this tendency appears to be continuing.

One research finding regarding ASL iconicity has proved to be highly reliable. Students of ASL who use the iconicity of signs as a rehearsal strategy report that it helps them remember the meaning of the signs that they wish to learn. But a word of caution is in order. The reported origins of ASL signs, even those cited in this text, may be fanciful inventions rather than historical facts. The sign AMERICA, illustrated in Figure 6, has been said to be derived from a log cabin, a split rail fence, and a melting pot. Obviously, not all of these suggestions can be correct. It may be helpful to students to associate a sign with a possible reason why it is made in a certain way, but they should be advised to take such associations with a grain of salt.

A special class of signs is initialized, that is, their handshape corresponds to the first letter of the English word that translates them.

Fig. 6. The sign AMERICA has been thought to be derived from a log cabin, a split rail fence, and a melting pot.

Examples are WATER, CHURCH, FAMILY, KING, LAW, It is tempting for hearing people to exploit this strategy so as to devise additional signs that will translate specific English words. For educational applications initialized signs have been invented for a very large number of English words, *e.g.*, IS, ARE, WAS, BE, SHE, HER, and even prefixes and suffixes, such as RE-, PRE-, -ING, -TION. Some of these newly developed signs have been used by school children for several years of training, and it seems likely that some of them may be absorbed into the ASL lexicon. This process may be accompanied by structural changes to accommodate ASL phonological rules. For example, the movement associated with the Signed English article, THE, is specified as a lateral movement to the right by authorities who use the system, but deaf children can be observed to alter that movement when the next sign is located at the forehead (THE MAN) or the left shoulder (THE KING). It also seems likely that some English forms are more likely to be found useful to deaf people using ASL than others. It is hard to imagine that signs like SHOULD or WOULD will ever become features of the ASL lexicon. However, only time will tell what effects currently popular language intervention systems may have on future ASL usage.

Students of ASL should exercise caution with respect to initialized signs. It may be tempting to invent new initialized signs for use with deaf people. But it is concepts, relations, and ideas that one should be translating into ASL, not English words. The sign HOSPITAL, for example, is executed with the "H" hand. The same execution with a "C" hand would not be likely to be recognized as a sign for *clinic*. Deaf people who use initialized signs may not even be aware of the fact that an English word is being referenced at the same time. This is especially true of young deaf children, whose sign vocabulary may be much larger and very different from their English language vocabulary.

The vocabulary of a living language evolves as needs arise for new symbols. ASL is a living language, and its lexicon is constantly changing. It took very little time for signs to be developed for ROCKET, STREAKER, BREAKDANCING, MACHO and FREEWAY. But it is very difficult to predict what motivation may prompt the formation of a new sign or which sign among alternatives will survive as the accepted usage. Several signs may evolve and be preserved in different communities as dialect differences. There are several different signs for SHOE, SANDWICH, and BIRTHDAY in use in various parts of the country. Students of ASL may long for a more logical and less diverse state of affairs. But living languages will always be changing and reflect diverse usages. That is one of the things that makes them interesting.

Noun/Verb Distinctions

Many nouns and verbs share important phonological features. For example, both FLY and AIRPLANE use the same hand configuration, and they are executed in the same approximate location. But FLY is executed as a single, relaxed movement, whereas AIRPLANE is executed is two or more tensed movements that cover only a very short distance. Similarly, the verb, TO TELEPHONE, CALL, lifts the "Y" hand from an imaginary cradle in neutral space and brings it up to the side of the head, with the thumb near the ear and the little finger near the mouth. The noun, TELEPHONE, moves the "Y" hand toward the side of the head with two or more brief, tensed movements. The same noun/verb distinction applies to a large number of signs that share phonological features but fall into a different form class: CUT *vs.* SCISSORS, SIT *vs.* CHAIR, EAT *vs.* FOOD, DRIVE *vs.* CAR, *etc*. It is important to discriminate the difference between nouns and verbs in ASL. The difference is usually marked by a single, longer, relaxed movement for verbs *vs.* two or more brief, tense movements for nouns.

Gender

Male and female gender are marked in ASL by the location of a sign's execution. Male signs are executed on or near the forehead, and female signs are executed on or near the right cheek and chin (Figure 7). These gender regions are probably derived from the signs invented by de l'Epee for the French articles *le* and *la*. The masculine article was executed by grasping the brim of an imaginary hat and lifting it. This sign survives in ASL as the sign BOY. The feminine gender was executed by tracing bonnet strings down the sides of the jaw. A remnant of this sign survives in ASL as the sign FEMALE, GIRL. (This latter sign is an example of a sign's loss of iconicity over time; no attempt is made today to "tie the bonnet," and without the above explanation it would be hard to imagine why a thumb stroked along the jaw would refer to GIRL.)

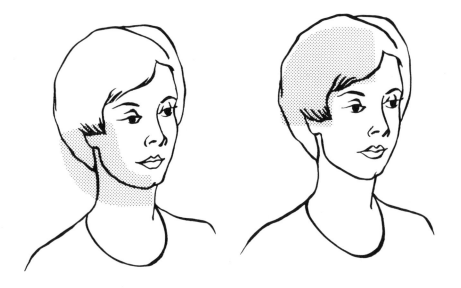

Fig. 7. Gender regions mark the difference between masculine and feminine nouns for many kinship signs.

Most kinship signs use the same handshape and movement for the male and female counterparts of relationships, but the gender region differs. The role of location as a distinctive feature for kinship signs can be readily observed by examining kinship pairs, *e.g.*, FATHER *vs.* MOTHER, SON *vs.* DAUGHTER, NEPHEW *vs.* NIECE, GRANDFA-THER *vs. GRANDMOTHER, HUSBAND vs. WIFE, and BROTHER vs. SISTER. AUNT and UNCLE are also signed in the appropriate gender region, but they differ in handshape as well as location, because they are initialized signs.*

Number

Nouns may be singular or plural. Unless they are pluralized by some specific means, they are typically construed as singular. Sometimes the context makes it obvious that a noun is to be taken as a plural. But when the context offers no clue, there are several ways to pluralize a noun. They will be discussed one at a time, but with no implication that one strategy is to be preferred over another. Finally, the appropriateness of the various strategies for different types of nouns will be discussed.

Some nouns appear in a plural idiomatic form. Examples are PEO-PLE and, perhaps, CHILDREN. Also falling into a special class are nouns like FOREST and CITY, which are derived from the signs TREE and HOUSE.

Any noun that is modified by an adjective that implies a plural number is to be considered a plural noun (Figure 8). Examples are MY CAR TWO, MY FRIEND GROUP, AIRPLANE MANY, TREE FEW, *etc.*

A noun can be pluralized by reduplicating it, usually in different locations. Thus, STREET STREET STREET = STREETS, GROUP GROUP GROUP = GROUPS, CHAIR CHAIR CHAIR = CHAIRS (Figure 9). One handed signs that are pluralized by reduplication may be executed with alternating right and left hands (ADULT, AIRPLANE).

A noun can be pluralized by indexing (THERE THERE THERE) as in Figure 10. If the index is made casually with no attention to precisely which or how many locations are specified, the plural does not carry with it any further implications. However, if the execution is deliberate, with eye gaze directed to the locations as they are specified, the message may include information with regard to the exact number and relative position of the referents. Thus, one can sign ME SEE CAR THERE THERE THERE to indicate *I see three cars, two near one another and a third some distance away.* Or one can sign ME HAVE TREE THERE THERE THERE THERE to indicate *I have a row of four trees.*

A noun may be pluralized by assigning it a classifier and then pluralizing the classifier. A classifier is a handshape that refers to a noun. (This definition implies that a classifier is a pronoun, and classifiers will

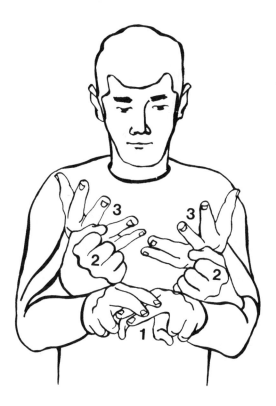

Fig. 8. Modifying a noun (CHAIR) with a plural adjective (MANY) pluralizes the noun.

be discussed further in the chapter on pronouns.) The handshape typically bears some resemblance to the noun to which the classifier refers, *e.g.*, a flat hand for flat objects, like BOOK or WALL, a raised index finger for vertical objects like a PERSON, raised fingers for several vertical objects, like PEOPLE, cupped hands for cylindrical objects, like CAN, an inverted "V" or bent "V" for the legs of a PERSON, the thumbs-up "3" hand for a VEHICLE, *etc.* A classifier can convey information about the relative position of a noun or nouns, as in ROW, CIRCLE, or LINE, or about the movement associated with one or more nouns as in AIRPLANE-TAKE-OFF-BANK-FLY-AWAY, VEHICLE-RUN-OFF-ROAD-INTO-DITCH, VEHICLE(1) PASS VEHICLE(2). Typically, a classifier is executed with the dominant hand, but both hands may be used to represent two classifiers at once, *e.g.*, a PERSON (right

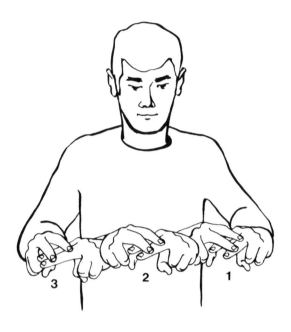

Fig. 9. CHAIR may be pluralized by reduplicating the execution in different locations.

inverted "V") astride a HORSE (left sideways "B").

How is a classifier pluralized? There are two general strategies. One involves a smooth movement, the other involves a reduplicated execution. The direction of the movement may convey information regarding the position of the plural referents. For example, to represent a row of books the sign BOOK could be followed by an execution which places both palms together in front of the body and then draws the dominant hand off to the right in a straight line. Three rows of books can be represented by repeating the plural classifier with each execution a bit below the previous one in space. If the classifier is executed vertically, it can represent a stack or stacks of books. Classifiers can be used to represent a row or rows of chairs (bent "V" hands, palms down), a row or rows or people ("4" hands), a line or lines of cars ("3" hands), a row or rows of cans ("C" hands), or a row of chairs (bent "V" hands) (Figure 11). If the "4" hands trace a circle, the execution implies a plural number of people in a circle. The "4" hands can represent a line that stretches from a ticket window down the street and around a corner.

Fig. 10. A noun may be pluralized by repeated indexing in different locations (CHAIR THERE THERE THERE).

A reduplicated execution of the classifier may also be used to pluralized its noun. Each pause in the series of executions represents another example of the noun. This strategy would work as well as a single, smooth movement to represent a row of chairs or a line of cars. It would be inappropriate, however, for a line of people represented by the "4" hand, since the four fingers already pluralize the noun.

These various alternatives for pluralizing nouns are not equally appropriate for all nouns. It is not likely that a body contact sign like SOLDIER would be reduplicated, or that abstract signs like IDEA would be represented by a classifier. Until a set of rules has been abstracted for an ASL corpus, decisions as to how a noun is to be pluralized will have to be made on an individual basis. Needless to say, fluent speakers of ASL make these decisions appropriately without conscious attention to the choice of a strategy.

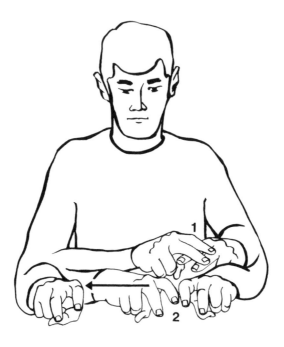

Fig. 11. A noun may be pluralized by assigning it a classifier and pluralizing the classifier (CHAIR + CL:ROW).

Case

Nouns take on various roles in a sentence. A noun may be the topic of a comment. A noun may be the subject of a sentence, the object of a verb, or an indirect object. In English the distinction between subjects, objects, and indirect objects is often made by means of word order. There is no ambiguity over who was shown to whom in the sentence, *I showed the policeman the robber.* Quite the opposite meaning is implied by *I showed the robber the policeman.* Just by looking at the words, *robber* and *policeman* it is impossible to tell who was shown to whom, but the word order makes it clear.

In ASL, sign order is not such a certain clue as to the intended meaning. Unless nonmanual features are added to a sentence, the meaning may be ambiguous. One of the more important nonmanual strategies available in ASL is spatial organization. If the robber is assigned a location off to the left and the policeman is assigned a location off to the right, the direction of movement of the sign SHOW will indicate clearly who was shown to whom. Other examples of directional verbs which may take both a direct and an indirect object are GIVE, THROW, WRITE, SEND, *etc.* Some directional verbs take a direct but not an indirect object (SEE, LOVE, MEET, HIT). Still other directional verbs are intransitive (LEAVE, FALL). When a verb is a directional verb, it must agree with the overall spatial organization of the message. When the listener becomes the speaker, the spatial organization established by the speaker is taken as the starting point for additional statements. Spatial organization is discussed elsewhere in this manual in connection with indexing as a pronominal reference and with verbs and their spatial agreement with localized nouns.

Common and Proper Nouns

Common nouns are used for referents that are not unique. A cup is a cup. Each cup is not distinguished from all other cups by its name. Proper names, on the other hand, are reserved for one-of-a-kind references. There is only one Poland, only one Rochester, NY, and only one Thomas Paine. One must not overdo this emphasis on uniqueness. November is a proper noun, and one comes around every year. Sundays come once a week. But there is still something unique about Sunday and November. They are different from the other days of the week or from the other months of the year.

ASL provides three means of representing proper nouns. First, they may be fingerspelled in their entirety. This is the common practice when the noun is infrequently used. Secondly, proper nouns may be indicated by means of fingerspelled signs (F-L-A, S-T-L, L-A, K-C). Thirdly, commonly used proper nouns tend to acquire name signs (NEW-YORK, MILWAUKEE, CALIFORNIA, NEW-ORLEANS). Members of the deaf community invent name signs for each other. In some countries these are iconic, reflecting a physical feature or characteristic of the person. In the U.S. name signs are typically initialized signs, with the first letter of person's first name tapped to their shoulder, chest, cheek, head, chin, *etc.*

Compound Nouns

Compounds are signs which are composed of two elements, each of which, by itself, may have a meaning of its own. But the compound has a meaning that is different from the two elements taken singly or together. Examples of English word compounds are *railroad, baseball, whiplash, etc.* Typically it is impossible to guess the meaning of the compound solely from knowing the elements that make it up. Examples of compounds in ASL are AGREE (THINK + SAME), HUSBAND (MAN + MARRY), and DAUGHTER (FEMALE + BABY). Compounds in

English are not pronounced the same way that the two separate words would be pronounced if they were to be taken literally. A *black bird* is pronounced differently than a *blackbird*. Similarly, compound signs are not signed in the same way as their component elements. They take less time than the two signs would take up if they were signed separately (THINK SAME *vs.* AGREE). Moreover, the handshape of the compound tends to be the same for the entire sign, even though the component elements would require different handshapes. The prevailing handshape typically comes from the second element of the compound. Thus, DAUGHTER uses the "B" hand for the entire sign.

Compounds are a useful device for generating new signs. A sign for STREAKER was developed as a compound from BARE and ZIP-AWAY. Their presence in ASL is an example of the productivity of the language, namely, its ability to generate new symbols with novel meanings.

Summary

A noun is a name of a person, place, or thing. Nouns occupy specific functions in ASL sentences. They may be subjects of verbs, objects of verbs, indirect objects, predicate nominatives, or objects of prepositions. They may also function as topics of comments. The comment may also include nouns in a variety of grammatical roles. Whether a noun is a topic, a subject, or an object in a sentence is indicated by the syntax of a sentence. In ASL, the syntax includes nonmanual features, such as spatial organization, which provide clues for interpreting the role of the nouns in the sentence.

Nouns may be common or proper. Common nouns may be singular or plural. There are a variety of strategies in ASL for pluralizing nouns, including modifying the noun with a plural adjective, reduplication, indexing, and assigning a classifier which is, then, pluralized. Which of these strategies is appropriate in a given circumstance will depend on the noun that is to be pluralized and on the situation or context. Nouns may be formed by inventing new signs, sometimes iconic, by developing fingerspelled signs, or by a process of compounding from existing signs.

Chapter Four: Pronouns in American Sign Language

Definitions

Pronouns stand in place of nouns. There are several kinds of pronouns: personal pronouns *(I, you, they, etc.)*, demonstrative pronouns *(this, that, these, those)*, reflexive pronouns *(myself, themselves, etc.)*, relative pronouns *(who, which, whose, etc.)*, indefinite pronouns *(each, any, both, etc.)*, and interrogative pronouns *(who? whose? whoever?, etc.)*. American Sign Language has pronouns, too. Sometimes they are executed as a specific sign, such as WE OUR, MY, or YOURSELF. Sometimes they take the form of an index. The simplest form of an index is for the speaker to point to an object within the listener's field of view. Alternatively, the speaker may gesture toward the object with the hand or arm or merely glance at the object. If the object is not physically present, the speaker may index a location in which the referent is imagined to be or where the referent is typically found. Sometimes pronouns are embedded in a directional verb (GIVE-ME) so that a specific sign for the pronoun (ME) does not occur at all; but it is there, nevertheless, in the directional execution of the verb. Finally, a specialized set of handshapes known as *classifiers* may be used as pronouns, or role taking may allow the speaker to become the referent and, thus, serve as a pronoun.

Personal Pronouns

Like English, ASL has signs for the personal pronouns. When they occur as the subject of a verb, they are signed as follows:

1st Person singular: INDEX-ME or Initialized I

2nd Person singular: INDEX-YOU

3rd Person singular: INDEX-HE, INDEX-SHE, INDEX-IT

1st Person plural: WE or Initialized WE

2nd Person plural: INDEX-YOU + lateral sweep or YOU, YOU, YOU (directional)

3rd Person plural: INDEX-THEY + lateral sweep or HE, HE, HE; SHE, SHE, SHE *etc.* (directional)

Most of the personal pronouns listed above are executed as an INDEX in ASL, that is, the speaker points to himself or herself for I or ME, to the listener or listeners for YOU, and to the referent or referents for HE, SHE, IT, and THEY. In ASL it is simply not true that it is impolite to point. The index finger is used for such pointing. For very formal indexing, the open hand may be used. It is stroked down the right side of the body for I or ME, moved gently downward in space as it is directed toward another person (YOU, HE, SHE) or moved laterally for THEY or YOU (plural). The exceptions to the rule that the personal pronouns are executed as an INDEX are the optional initialized I and WE for the first person singular and plural. Even the standard first person plural is derived from indexing the subject by touching the right shoulder, sweeping the index around to enclose a plural number of people, and then indexing the subject again, this time on the left shoulder. Over time this execution has been reduced to a less iconic sign: the index finger is merely touched to the right and left shoulder.

When the personal pronoun occurs as the object of a verb or the object of a preposition, most of the forms are the same as when they are the subjects of the verb. For example, the sign HIM is the same as the sign HE: an INDEX directed toward the referent or toward the location where the referent is imagined to be. The exception is the initialized US. There are two variants for US, one executed with the extended fingers of the "U" hand pointed upward and one with the extended fingers pointed downward.

In the possessive form, the open palm is used instead of the index finger (Figure 12). MY, MINE (palm against the chest) YOUR, YOURS (palm directed toward the listener) HIS, HER, HERS, ITS (palm directed toward the referent) OUR, OURS (thumb edge of palm touched to the right shoulder and moved in an arc so that the little finger edge of the palm touches the left shoulder) YOUR, YOURS (pl.) (palm directed toward the listeners in a lateral movement) THEIR, THEIRS (palm directed toward the referents in a lateral movement).

There is a dual personal pronoun, WE TWO, YOU TWO, THEY TWO, executed with the extended index and middle fingers, palm up. There is also a special execution for WE THREE, YOU THREE, THEY THREE and WE FOUR, YOU FOUR, THEY FOUR involving the "3" hand and the "4" hand, respectively. The sign WE TWO, *etc.*, is moved

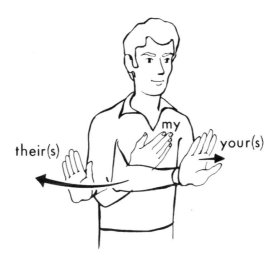

their(s)   my   your(s)

Fig. 12. The possessive pronoun uses the open palm in a directional execution.

back and forth between the referents. WE THREE and WE FOUR executes a circle which includes the speaker. For YOU THREE or THEY FOUR the circle is executed away from the speaker's body so as to exclude the speaker from the group. Multiple indexing to reference a plural number of pronouns is illustrated in Figure 13.

Reflexive Pronouns

The reflexive pronoun uses a special handshape, namely, a closed fist with a raised thumb. The various forms are executed as follows:

MYSELF (back of thumb and fist tapped against the chest)
YOURSELF (ball of thumb directed toward the listener)
HIMSELF, HERSELF, ITSELF (ball of thumb directed toward the referent)
OURSELVES (back of thumb touched against the right and left shoulder)
YOURSELVES (ball of thumb directed toward the listeners in a lateral movement)
THEMSELVES (ball of thumb directed toward the referents in a lateral movement)

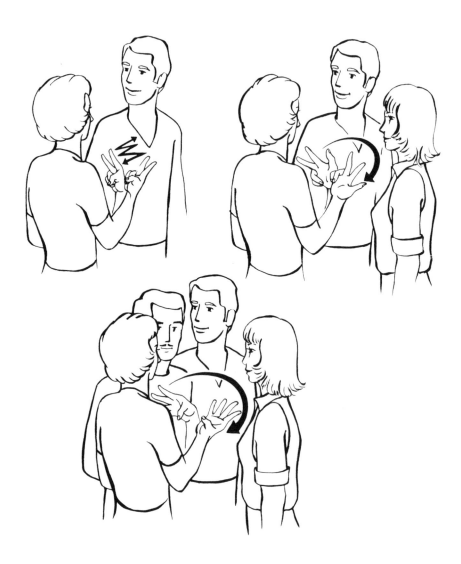

Fig. 13. Multiple indexing provides pronouns for duals (WE-TWO) triads (WE-THREE), and groups of four (WE-FOUR).

The reflexive pronoun is used in ASL in ways that are similar to English, HE HURT HIMSELF. But there are also unique emphatic uses that have yet to be carefully analyzed in a large corpus of ASL. One example occurs in *Deaf Models of ASL:* SHOULD HIMSELF LEARN. This may be translated into English, *He should learn for himself,* or *He should learn to be independent.*

Interrogative Pronouns

Interrogative pronouns in ASL make use of specific signs. There are signs for the interrogative WHO? WHICH? and WHAT? Two of these, WHICH and WHAT, may also be used as interrogative adjectives (WHICH WAY? WHAT TIME?). The possessive and objective forms of WHO? (WHOSE? WHOM?) are the same as the nominative case. These pronouns may be used as the comment following a topic, *e.g.,* BIRTHDAY: WHO? *(Whose birthday is it?)* or FOOTBALL: WHO WIN? *(Who won the football game?).* In some cases a statement may serve as the topic of the interrogative, *e.g.,* YOU GIVE BOOK: (INDEX) WHO? *(To whom did you give the book?)* or YOU WANT COFFEE TEA: WHICH? *(Which do you want, coffee or tea?).* In the case of the interrogative, WHICH?, the alternatives may be assigned different locations adjacent to each other in neutral space. In the example above, COFFEE could be signed slightly to the left of center, and TEA could be signed slightly to the right of center. The sign WHICH? could then be executed so that each hand were in the approximate location of one of the alternatives. The listener can make his choice by pointing to the appropriate location.

Demonstrative Pronouns

The demonstrative pronoun in ASL uses the right "Y" hand. For the singular, THIS, THAT, the dominant "Y" hand is struck against the nondominant palm or directed toward the referent, real or imagined. THIS is likely to be executed in neutral space near the body, and THAT is likely to be directed away from the body. The plural forms move the right "Y" hand laterally, near the body for THESE, away from the body for THOSE. The motion may be smooth, indicating a plural number in a general way, or it may be directed at specific locations, indicating specific references, *e.g.,* THIS, THIS, THIS, THIS for THESE.

Relative Pronouns

Relative pronouns are used very frequently in English. Examples of relative pronouns found in English are *who, which,* and *what.* Some of these are inflected. *Who* and *which* have a possessive form, *whose,* and *who* has an objective form, *whom.* Needless to say, ASL does not inflect these pronouns in the same manner as English. Ordinarily an INDEX serves as a relative pronoun for a previous noun. An index may establish a location for a noun, and this location may, then, be used for subsequent pronominal references. Thus, in English one might say, *I know a man who can help me*, but in ASL one could say, ME KNOW MAN THERE; INDEX-HE CAN HELP ME. The INDEX-HE, serves in this case as the relative pronoun, *who*. The antecedent, MAN, may be marked with a head movement which marks it for subsequent reference by a relative pronoun.

A possessive pronoun is used for the possessive form. For the English, *I know a man whose car is stuck*, one could say ME KNOW MAN; HIS CAR STUCK. As before, when a pronoun is to follow relating back to MAN, a head movement may mark MAN as the antecedent.

In addition to the nonmanual link between the antecedent (marked with a head nod) and the relative pronoun, relative clauses can be subordinated in ASL by means of other nonmanual features, such as the facial expression and body stance or the location and emphasis associated with their execution. The specific nonmanual marker of a relative clause is complex. It includes a brow raise, a backward tilt of the head, and a contraction of the muscles of the cheek raising the upper lip.

The following is an example of an INDEX used as a personal pronoun (ME) and a relative pronoun (HE). In addition, there are pronouns embedded in the directional verbs: (ASK-HIM, GIVE-ME).

INDEX-ME KNOW MAN; INDEX-HE RICH. THINK INDEX-ME ASK-HIM (directional) GIVE-ME (directional) MONEY.

This would be translated into English as *I know a man who is rich. I think I will ask him to give me money.*

Indefinite Pronouns

Indefinite pronouns are like demonstratives in that they refer to nouns, but they do so less clearly or less specifically. There are signs for a number of indefinite pronouns: EACH, EVERY, SOME, OTHER, ANOTHER, ANY, EITHER, BOTH, NONE, ALL, SEVERAL, FEW, MANY, ONE-ANOTHER. Several of these may be used as adjectives (SOME PEOPLE, ANY TIME, MANY YEARS) as well as substantives (SOME CAN, ME LIKE ANY, MANY KNOW).

Role Taking as a Pronominal Reference.

Thus far two major pronominal forms have been presented, indexes, which point to a real or imagined referent, and specific signs, such as ME, YOUR, HIMSELF, *etc.*, which represent a noun. There are other strategies for pronominal reference in ASL that are not generally considered to be pronouns in English. Two of them will be discussed here in some detail. The first is role taking.

ASL discourse includes narration, in which the speaker refers to one or more characters who have roles to play in the narrative. In telling a story, for example, one might refer to Cinderella, perhaps inventing a name sign for her, to her two step sisters and her wicked step mother, to the fairy godmother, the king and the prince. The narrative also requires a reference to a pumpkin that became a coach, to some mice that became the horses, and to a rat that became the coachman. An important object, a slipper, is also likely to be referenced. Thus, a narrative such as this has ample justification for the use of a large number of pronouns. The alternative would be to repeat the nouns, and that would be monotonous.

In English, such a narrative would make frequent use of personal pronouns, such as *she, they, he, it.* In ASL, role taking can eliminate the need for such verbal reminders of who is speaking or acting. The speaker can take the role of referent, and everything the narrator says or does is construed as being said or done by the referent. Thus, when the fairy godmother gives Cinderella instructions to gather the assortment of materials that will become her carriage, and when she waves her magic wand, the pronominal reference is accomplished by the narrator assuming the role of the fairy godmother. The godmother's statements are direct quotes, and her actions are carried out as if the speaker were an actor or actress playing the role. In effect, the speaker's body functions as a pronoun, referencing the fairy godmother and what she said and did. The speaker can then take the role of Cinderella and indicate what she said and did. Such role changes are not announced. The listener is expected to read nonmanual cues as to the identity of the agent that the speaker is representing.

In the text, *The American Sign Language,* role taking as a pronominal reference is introduced in the narrative involving a doctor and patient (p. 31-32.). The doctor gave the patient (the narrator) instructions, which the patient accepted. DOCTOR SAY "STAY HOME. COME SEE ME, OK; OTHER OUT, NO. NOT LISTEN, GO HOSPITAL." The pronominal reference to the doctor is accomplished by the narrator taking the role of the doctor and issuing these instructions with an air of authority.

Role taking is not limited to human characters. A narrator in ASL can imitate a bird or an animal, or even a mechanical toy or machine. Examples of English sentences that can be translated into ASL using role taking for the pronominal reference include the following:

The dog looked both ways before crossing the street.

DOG: LOOK (left), LOOK (right); CROSS.

A mechanical monster marched out and stabbed at me.

(MECHANICAL-MONSTER (sign mime) WALK STAB)(*I Want to Talk*, p. 68.)

The narrator's switch from one role to the other may be very abrupt with only minimal cues that a pronominal reference is taking place. In exaggerated examples the narrator may change the facial expression, the body stance, and even the body orientation to signal that a different person is speaking. For example, a child speaking to an adult will look up, perhaps with a pleading expression, whereas an adult speaking to a child will look down, perhaps in ASL, with pronominal references accomplished by taking the role of one or the other character in the narrative. But such exaggeration is unusual. Ordinarily the listener will have to be able to detect minimal cues that the narrator is switching roles.

Classifiers

Thus far three strategies for pronominal references have been described, namely, indexing, specific signs, and role taking. The fourth strategy for pronominal referencing in ASL to be discussed here is the use of classifiers.

Classifiers are handshapes which bear at least some resemblance to the noun to which they refer and which can be used in place of the noun to communicate information about its position or its movement. The resemblance between a classifier and its noun can be made clear with a few examples. A classifier for a CAN would use a cupped hand, whereas a classifier for a BOOK would use a flat palm. Other objects that might be represented by a cupped hand are a GLASS, a CUP, a TRASH-CAN, or a BOTTLE. Other objects that might be represented by a flat hand are a WALL, DOOR, BOARD, PANEL, or SHEET-OF-PAPER. Other handshapes that are frequently used as classifiers are the raised index finger for vertical objects (PERSON, POLE), the thumb-up fist for less slender, vertical objects (FLOWER-POT, BOTTLE, TREE, HOUSE, BUSH) the inverted "V" (representing legs) (MAN, WOMAN, DUCK, DOLL, HORSE, DOG, etc.), and the thumb-up "3" hand for a vehicle (CAR, HELICOPTER, SHIP). More specialized classifiers are the extended thumb, index, and little finger for AIRPLANE, four extended fingers for a plural number of PEOPLE, the bent "V" hand, palm down, for a seated person or stationary animal, and the curved fingers of the hand, palm down, for some kind of INSECT or ANIMAL.

The human hand is a very flexible instrument for representing a variety of actions and movements. One of the functions of a classifier is to represent by means of the handshape the agent of an action and then to portray the action with the movement of the hand. Thus, Mike Barry in *I Want to Talk* (p. 53 ff.) used classifiers to represent a roller coaster, bump-em cars, a carnival ride up a hill, a double-decker merry-go-round, a carnival ride through a dark tunnel, or a carnival ride down a slide into a pool of water. Using the classifier for a vehicle one can represent a car weaving down the road, pulling off the road, driving into a ditch, or backing up and going in the opposite direction. Using the classifier for an airplane one can represent a plane taking off, landing, or performing stunts. The index finger can represent a person moving toward the speaker, past the speaker, away from the speaker, and complex combinations of such movements.

Since a speaker has two hands, a dual is easy to execute using classifiers. Some signs seem to be derived from such dual executions, *e.g.*, MEET, FOLLOW, CONTEST, AVOID, CHASE, RACE, or PASS. Using the classifier for a vehicle, the dual execution can represent one car following another, passing another, or crashing into another. The raised index fingers of each hand can represent two people approaching each other and stopping before they meet, passing each other going in opposite directions, or walking down an aisle together. Curved "V" hands (SIT) can represent two people seated side by side *vs.* two people seated opposite each other, as in Figure 14, or two people sitting close together *vs.* two people sitting far apart. This strategy is not restricted to executions in which both hands present the same handshape. Two different classifiers can be presented simultaneously, *e.g.*, a man riding a horse, a car hitting a wall, a child on a merry-go-round, or a person sitting on a wall.

Classifiers may be pluralized in one of two ways. In the one case, both hands are needed with the same handshape on both hands. The dominant hand is drawn away from the nondominant hand in a smooth motion. This strategy is typically used for things like a row of cans ("C" hands), a shelf of books (palms), a row of chairs (curved "V" hands), a line of cars ("3" hands), or a line of people ("4" hands). It may be noted that the direction of the movement conveys information about the spatial arrangement of the objects, that is, whether they are a row (a lateral movement) or a line (a movement back toward the speaker's body).

The second pluralization strategy amounts to a reduplication, that is, the classifier is placed in more than one location. This can be done with one hand or with both. An example of a one-handed plural execution using the thumb-up fist is the following, where CL stands for the classifier executed in several different locations:

TREE: CL, CL, CL, CL.

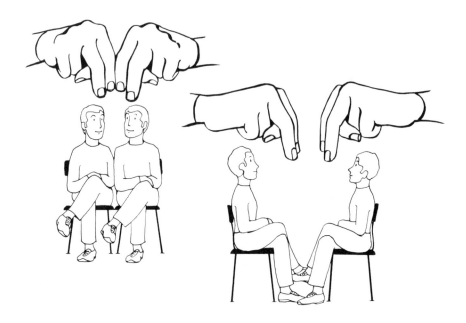

Fig. 11. Dual classifiers can represent two people sitting side by side or two people sitting across from each other.

It should be noted that the placement of the classifier conveys additional information about the spatial arrangement of the referent. If the placements are orderly and in a row, one would translate, *There is a row of trees* or *There are four trees lined up in a row*. If the placements are relatively random, without specific attention to how many or where they are placed, one might translate, *There are trees scattered about*. The relative placement of classifiers can indicate that the population of items is dense or sparse, organized in a pattern or in disarray, or in a straight, curved, or angled line. Other examples of spatial information communicated by means of classifiers are a circle of people, a semi-circle of chairs, or a double line of trees.

The two major items of information that are likely to conveyed by a classifier are, first, the position or spatial arrangement of the object or objects or, second, the movement of the object or objects. Sometimes both arrangement and movement may be indicated, *e.g.*, rows of marching soldiers, one car following and then passing the other, or people meeting and then going away side by side.

Implied Pronouns *Incorporated*

Not all pronouns are explicitly executed. Some are implied by the direction of the execution. For example, to translate, *Give the book to him,* into ASL, one could use an index for both the book and the pronoun, him: BOOK INDEX-IT GIVE INDEX-HIM. But to do that one has to have a location in mind where HE is located. In that case, the index is superfluous, since one can execute the verb, GIVE, in the direction of that location: BOOK INDEX-IT GIVE-HIM (directional). The directional execution would be translated into English, *Give the book to him.* Other directional verbs that can imply pronouns are LOOK-AT, illustrated in Figure 15, *(Look at me, Look at him)*, and SHOW *(Show him, Show me).*

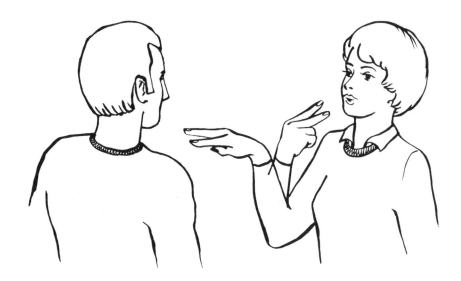

Fig. 15. Directional verbs can imply a pronoun as the object: LOOK-AT-YOU, LOOK-AT-ME.

Even signs that are not ordinarily directional can, nevertheless, imply a pronominal reference by the way in which they are executed. If a CHAIR is identified as a topic, the verb PAINT can imply IT as the object by executing the verb as if a chair were imagined to be the object of the action. Other verbs that can imply a pronominal reference are EAT (an apple), PEEL (a banana), THROW (a football), and SWAT (a fly). In the latter instance, eye gaze (an INDEX?) may assist the verb in tracking and, thereby, implying that the fly is the object of the verb.

Translation is sometimes a matter of taste and style, and a pronoun may not always be considered to be necessary as part of the translation. But if a translator makes use of a pronoun to render the sense of the original, the translator can appeal for support to the direction or the manner of execution of the verb.

Summary

There are four specific devices in ASL for executing pronouns. First, there are specific signs for certain pronouns, *e.g.*, WE (personal), MYSELF (reflexive), THIS (demonstrative), WHO? (interrogative), EACH (indefinite). Secondly, an index can be used as a pronominal reference, sometimes pointing to the referent and sometimes pointing to a location where the referent is imagined to be located. Thirdly, by taking the role of an imagined referent, the speaker can use his or her own body as a pronoun. Statements are, then, construed as direct quotes, and actions are construed as acts of the referent. Fourthly, classifiers may stand in place of nouns and communicate information about the position or the movement of the referent or referents. Classifiers are especially versatile pronouns, since they can be singular, dual, or plural, and since they can represent either spatial locations, spatial relations, or movements with a single execution.

In addition to these four devices, pronouns may be implied by the directional execution of verbs such as GIVE, LOOK, SHOW. These are transitive verbs, taking an object. When the object is imagined to be present in a specific location, and when these verbs are executed toward that location, the directional execution implies a pronominal reference to that object. Even the manner of execution of a verb may imply a pronominal reference, as when a transitive verb is executed with an imaginary object in mind.

Chapter Five: Verbs in American Sign Language

Definition

The verb is the key element in the predicate of a sentence. It describes what the subject does. Sometimes the verb can stand alone, as in CAR LEAVE. Usually the verb requires a complement. The complement can be a direct object, a prepositional phrase, an infinitive construction, or any other word, phrase, or clause that completes the predicate.

Tense

The verb in ASL can be expressed in the past, present, or future tense. To mark the tense of verbs, the speaker typically establishes a temporal frame of reference for a passage or a segment of discourse by means of a specific sign. The signs which refer to tense make use of a spatial frame of reference that can be described relative to the location of the speaker's body. A time line can be imagined to run horizontally across the front of the body, as in Figure 16. The present tense is right on the time line, as in the sign, NOW. Signs for the past are located behind the time line, and signs for the future are in front of the time line. The signs used for the past, present, and future are generally glossed AGO, PAST for the past tense, NOW for the present tense, and WILL, FUTURE for the future tense. Examples of ASL sentences with a temporal frame of reference established for the verbs are as follows:

LONG TIME AGO ME LIVE WASHINGTON.

A long time ago I lived in Washington.

NOW ME LIVE OHIO.

Now I live in Ohio.

FUTURE ME LIVE CALIFORNIA.

I will live in California.

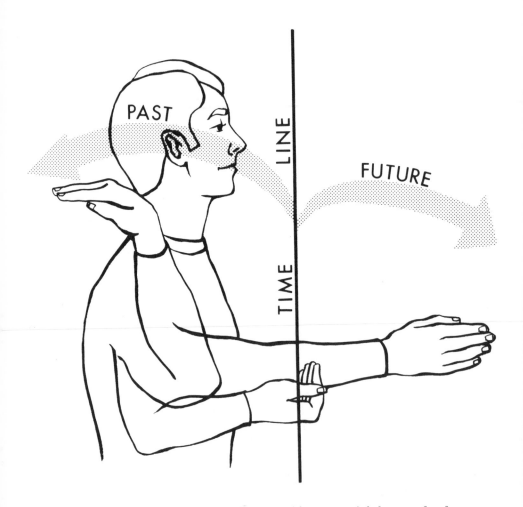

Fig. 16. A vertical time line provides a spatial frame of reference for the past, present, and future.

Often the sign for the temporal frame of reference is the first sign to be executed, marking all the signs that follow as past, present, or future. The following are examples of sentences in which a single marker for tense affects all the verbs that follow:

AGO ME LIVE WASHINGTON. ME WORK GALLAUDET COL-
LEGE. ME GO SCHOOL CATHOLIC UNIVERSITY.

I used to live in Washington. I worked at Gallaudet College. I went to school at Catholic University.

FUTURE MY CHILDREN GROW UP, LEAVE HOME. MAYBE THEY MARRY, HAVE CHILDREN. ME BECOME GRANDFA-THER.

My children will grow up and leave home. Maybe they will marry and have children. I will become a grandfather.

Although the sign indicating tense usually appears first in a passage or narrative, it may appear later. The following are examples:

ME SEE DOCTOR AGO. DOCTOR SAY ME FINE.

I saw the doctor. He said I was fine.

ME GO NEW YORK VACATION FUTURE. ME STAY TWO WEEK

I will go to New York for a vacation. I will stay two weeks.

Notice that in the above examples the verbs, unlike English verbs, are not inflected as are English verbs with special endings or helping verbs to mark their tense. Their English translation, however, will make use of helping verbs or inflections that are appropriate in English to reflect the intended tense of the verbs.

The signs for PAST and FUTURE may be modified to refer to the recent past, A-LITTLE-WHILE-AGO, RECENTLY, and the imminent future, IN-A-LITTLE-WHILE, SHORTLY. One or more of the following nonmanual features are used for this modification: shoulders hunched together, squinted eyes, twisted mouth (Figure 17). In addition, the location of the execution is closer to the cheek, and the distance of the movement is greatly reduced, and the execution may be reduplicated. For RECENTLY there are two variants, one with the palm moved back toward the shoulder near the cheek with one or more of the nonmanual features named above or the raised right index finger wiggled backward near the right cheek with one or more of the nonmanual features named above. For SHORTLY the sign FUTURE is executed with an abbreviated movement reduplicated near the cheek with one or more of the nonmanual features named above.

A similar inflection can be applied to the present tense, as well. NOW can be signed very close to the chest with the mouth pulled so as to show some teeth and with squinted eyes to mean JUST-NOW. Verbs can be assigned the same inflection, *e.g.,* ARRIVE, LEAVE, COME, VISIT, *etc.* to mean *I just arrived, He just left, She just came, I just visited [there], etc.*

The signs for PAST and FUTURE may be modified so as to refer to the REMOTE-PAST, LONG-AGO, or the REMOTE-FUTURE, A-

LONG-TIME-FROM-NOW (Figure 17). Nonmanual cues include some combination of relaxed muscle tone, a slowed rate of of execution, and a relaxed and open mouth. The movement is extended far forward for REMOTE-FUTURE and far back over the shoulder for REMOTE-PAST. Alternatively, both hands can be rolled over one another backward over the right shoulder for REMOTE-PAST.

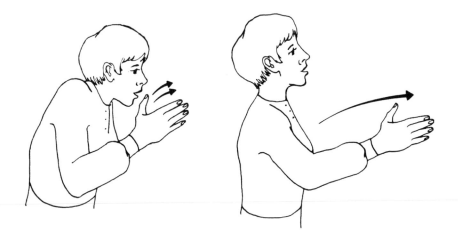

Fig. 17. Future temporal adverbs can be modified to imply the imminent future (left panel) or the remote future (right panel).

Within the spatial dimensions set for the REMOTE-PAST and the REMOTE-FUTURE, gradations can be represented by using more or less of the total space within reach. For example, if the right arm is extended as far as possible, this would imply a more remote time than if the right arm was extended to a point somewhere between that and a simple FUTURE. Meanwhile, nonmanual cues can also serve to accentuate the expanse of time implied by the execution, e.g., tilting the head, squinting the eyes, and beginning the execution very slowly, speeding it up only at the very end.

In addition to the basic signs for PAST, PRESENT and FUTURE, there are three other signs that make a specific temporal reference: SINCE, FINISH, and NOT-YET. Examples follow.

SINCE refers to an action which began in the past and continues to the present. It may be derived from the sign for HAPPEN. The same handshapes are involved, but the movement extends from above the right shoulder to neutral space, in effect a movement from the past (over the shoulder) to the present (in front of the body). In some contexts the sign may be glossed UNTIL NOW. The sign sentence SINCE THREE YEAR ME WORK NEWSPAPER would be translated *For three years I have been working at the newspaper*, or *I have been working for the newspaper for three years.*

FINISH refers to an action completed in the past. This is not the only use for FINISH in ASL. It can take on a variety of meanings, and it is used in a large number of idioms, such as the imperative, FINISH! meaning *Stop that*, or FINISH TOUCH for *I have been there*. But when it is used as a temporal reference, it clearly implies a completed past action. In some contexts it can be glossed OVER, DONE. Examples of Sign sentences using FINISH to establish tense are ME EAT FINISH for *I have eaten*, BASEBALL FINISH for *The baseball game is over*, and ME SEE MOVIE FINISH for *I saw the movie.*

NOT-YET refers to an action which has yet to occur. It may be related to the sign LATE, as both are signed with the same hand configuration in the same location and with essentially the same movement. LATE, however, is generally executed as a single larger movement backward at the side of the body with the lower right forearm, while NOT-YET is a reduplicated execution executed with a backward movement from the wrist. In ASL discourse the sign may occur, for example, in YOU EAT YOU? (Answer) NOT-YET, or MY FRIEND ME NOT-YET SEE HIM for *I have not yet seen my friend.*

There are many adverbs which will cause the verbs that they modify to be construed as a past, present, or future tense. For example, adverbs that may mark the past tense include YESTERDAY, LAST-WEEK, TWO-WEEKS-AGO, LAST-YEAR, TWO-YEAR-AGO, NEVER, *etc.* Adverbs that may mark the present tense are NOW, ALWAYS, REGULARLY, EVERY-DAY, WEEKLY, YEARLY, OFTEN, SOMETIMES and TRULY. Adverbs that may mark the future tense include TOMORROW, NEXT-WEEK, TWO-WEEKS-FROM-NOW, NEXT-YEAR, TWO-YEARS-FROM-NOW, *etc.*

Once a verb is modified by a temporal adverb, subsequent verbs are construed in the same frame of reference. For example, YESTERDAY ME GO TOWN, BUY NEW CLOTHES would be translated with both verbs in the past tense: *Yesterday I went to town and bought new clothes.*

Some signs for marking PAST or FUTURE use the nondominant hand as a point of reference (PREVIOUSLY, LATER). If a temporal reference is to be embedded in a sentence in which an over-all temporal frame of reference remains intact, signs using the nondominant hand are required. For example, taken by itself, LATER ME EAT would be translated, *I will eat later*. Embedded in another context, YESTERDAY

ME GO SHOPPING, LATER ME SEE DOCTOR, we would translate, *Yesterday I went shopping, and afterward I saw a doctor.* Thus, within this established context, LATER, AFTERWARD allows the subsequent verb to be translated in the past, in keeping with the over-all temporal frame of reference. If the FUTURE sign were used instead of LATER, the sentence would be ambiguous. It could be translated, *Yesterday I went shopping; in the future I will see a doctor.*

Explicit signs for the tense of verbs are not always necessary. When the situation establishes a temporal frame of reference, additional signs, although permissible, are not necessary. In some cases they would be considered inappropriate; for example, if a child were to show up all covered with mud, and the mother said WHAT HAPPEN?, no one would construe the verb, HAPPEN, as anything but a past tense.

To summarize, verbs in ASL may be expressed in the past, present, or future tenses. The past and future may be modified with nonmanual features to refer to the near term past or future and to the long term past or future. There are specific signs for a past, present, or future temporal frame of reference, and there are specific signs for actions which began in the past and continue to the present, actions which are completed in the past, and actions which have not yet occurred. A large number of adverbs may also mark verbs as past, present, or future, and, by doing so, establish a temporal frame of reference for subsequent verbs. Temporal markers using the nondominant hand may be used to embed a temporal reference within an overall frame of reference that remains unchanged. Finally, the tense of verbs may be determined by the situation.

Directional Verbs

When spatial organization is used syntactically, verbs capable of being executed in more than one direction must agree spatially with the nouns that have been assigned locations. Examples of such verbs are GIVE, GO/COME, LEAVE, SHOW, TELL, INTRODUCE, DRIVE, SEND, THROW, LOOK-AT, TELL, SAY-NO, and QUESTION. The eye gaze may complement the spatial organization by including the imagined referents in the field of vision, referencing them at appropriate times during the discourse. Although for the purposes of linguistic description the spatial agreement that is required of certain verbs is generally said to be among the locations established for referents, it is clear from the way in which these locations are used that the nouns are imagined to be in these locations, and the verbs act on imaginary referents, not on locations. For example, a ball may be indexed as lying on the ground, but when the verb THROW occurs, the handshape accommodates to the size and shape of the ball, and before it is executed, a downward reach may retrieve the ball from that location so as to throw it.

The speaker's location is ordinarily fixed by the setting (unless role taking puts the person of the speaker in some other location), and signs directed toward the speaker will move toward the speaker, sometimes making contact. Thus, GIVE-ME brings the clustered fingers in an arc toward the chest, and GIVE-HIM extends the clustered fingers in an arc toward the location agreed upon for HIM. The qualification "agreed upon" is important, since speaker and listener must share the coordinated spatial relations that are constructed during a speaking episode. Typically, the speaker establishes these locations one by one as they are needed in a discourse, but as speaker and listener take turns in a conversation, the listener may accept the speaker's locations and, then, add others as new nouns are introduced into the discussion or narrative. Similarly, nouns may move or be moved about, exchange places, or come and go, and the spatial referents to them, whether pronouns or directional verbs, will keep track of their movements and relocations. It is well known that human memory for spatial relations is quite good, and ASL takes advantage of this human capacity in its reliance on spatial organization as an important aspect of its syntax.

When a directional verb references more than one noun, the execution is altered so as to include the additional references, either by a reduplicated execution in discrete locations or by an execution characterized by a horizontal sweep. Which of these strategies will be used generally depends on the verb. For example, to DRIVE to different locations requires a reduplicated execution, whereas LOOK-AT or GIVE can be performed with discreet or with sweeping movements. When either strategy is permitted by the verb, the choice will depend on the meaning that is to be conveyed.

Certain verbs allow for a dual directional execution. For example, each hand can represent a different agent, and the execution GIVE can mean that they exchanged gifts (Figure 18), SEND that they exchanged letters, and THROW that they were playing catch. The alternating, directional executions imply dual agents in each of these cases. Some signs that are now considered to be a part of the ASL lexicon may be based on such a construction, e.g., QUARREL, GOSSIP, CORRESPOND, DISCUSS.

Even verbs that are ordinarily executed in neutral space may be executed elsewhere so as to include a referent in the direction of their execution. Thus, the imperatives, FINISH, SIT, STOP, WORK, HURRY, STAY, etc. are generally aimed at the person to whom the command is being issued. When body contact prevents the directional execution of an imperative, either an explicit index or eye gaze link the

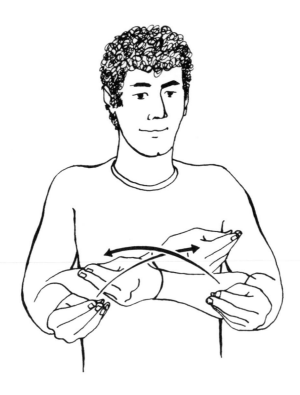

Fig. 18. Dual executions of directional verbs may imply reciprocal actions, such as EXCHANGE-GIFTS.

verb to the person to whom the command is given. Examples of verbs in which there is a restraint imposed by body contact are EAT, FORGET, ACCEPT, THINK, *etc*. A directional index may be executed with the nondominant hand at the same time that any one-handed verb is executed.

Some directional executions avoid referencing a specific location and, instead, imply an aimless or inattentive activity. In this case, the eye gaze often deliberately references a different location than the verb. English translations of verbs that may be executed in this way (LOOK,

GO, THROW) include *Look around aimlessly, go to various places,* and *discard.* Since it is the lack of agreement between eye gaze and directional execution that implies the casual, inattentive manner of executing the verb, it follows that the ordinary directional execution of a verb usually involves a complementary eye gaze. Subtle differences in meaning can depend on the coordination of directional execution and eye gaze. For example, a reduplicated GIVE in successive locations referenced by eye gaze implies a deliberate hand-out of some object to specific individuals, whereas the same execution without the eye gaze may merely imply that an unspecified number of objects was handed out. SIT executed in a vague semicircle may imply that everyone should sit down.

To summarize, verbs that can agree spatially with the spatial organization imposed on ASL discourse must do so. In particular, verbs must agree spatially with their subjects and objects or indirect objects. The agreement can be with dual subjects and with a plural number of subjects or objects. The spatial arrangement of referents may change during the course of a conversation, and the spatial agreement of verbs must reflect such changes. Eye gaze may complement the spatial agreement, or, conversely, lack of a complementary eye gaze may imply an indefinite number of referents with which the verb agrees.

Verbs and Classifiers

Classifiers typically convey two types of information about referents: (1) their location or spatial arrangement, and (2) their movement. The second of these implies a verb. For example, various movements of the handshape that serves as the classifier for a vehicle can imply all of the following verbs: WEAVE-DOWN-THE-ROAD, RUN-OFF-THE-ROAD-INTO-A-DITCH, DRIVE-OVER-A-HILL, PULL-OFF-THE-ROAD, BACK-UP, TURN-LEFT, TURN-RIGHT, *etc.* With the other hand serving as a classifier for another vehicle, the execution can imply the verbs: FOLLOW, PASS, LAG-BEHIND, COLLIDE-HEAD-ON, COLLIDE-BROADSIDE, COLLIDE-FROM-THE-REAR, PROCEED-SIDE-BY-SIDE, *etc.*

Several verbs that are considered to be part of the ASL lexicon may, in fact, be composed of the movement of classifiers. Consider the following:

Classifier: Index Finger(s). MEET, APPROACH-ME, (Dual) PASS-BY-EACH-OTHER.

Classifier: Thumb(s) up. FOLLOW, AVOID, CHASE, CONTEST, COMMUTE, PASS, LAG-BEHIND

Classifier: Inverted "V". STAND, JUMP, FALL, KNEEL, WALK, DANCE.

The representation of verbs by means of classifiers is a very versatile and productive strategy in ASL for communicating a variety of information about the actions of agents. A complex sequence of movements can be enacted with a classifier representing a complex sequence of actions by an agent. For example, two raised index fingers can represent two people approaching each other, stopping face to face, turning, and going away side by side. Two vehicle classifiers can portray a police car pulling another vehicle over to the side of the road. Two thumbs up classifiers can show a photo finish of a 100 meter dash.

Sign Mime

If classifiers can represent nouns and, by their movements, imply verbs, so can any other pronoun. Even an index can imply a verb if it follows a moving object, *e.g.*, a toy race car that goes round and round on a track, (see *I Want to Talk*, p. 93-94). But that is a relatively specialized and infrequent recourse in ASL. More commonly the speaker carries out the action as sign mime. In effect, the speaker's body becomes a pronoun, representing the noun who is the agent of the action, and the speaker's actions are interpreted as the agent's actions. Whatever the speaker says is a direct quote. Like the use of classifiers, sign mime is a versatile and productive strategy in ASL for expressing a great many verbs.

There are two general types of sign mime: hand mime and body mime. In hand mime the scale is reduced, as the dominant hand represents the agent and carries out the action in neutral space. The nondominant hand may represent the plane on which the action occurs as the dominant hand represents the agent and carries out the action. An example of hand mime is the sign SCRAPE, BULLDOZE, where the dominant hand represents the blade of a bulldozer, and the nondominant hand represents the ground over which the blade is scraping. In body mime the scale is generally life-size, and the action is performed using imaginary objects. An example of body mime is CHOP-WOOD, where the speaker holds an imaginary axe and swings it down at an imaginary piece of wood.

Many signs that are generally considered to be part of the ASL lexicon can be traced to hand mime or body mime for their origins. For example, many of the signs that refer to a sport (FISH, HUNT, GOLF, PLAY-TENNIS, BOWL, SWIM, PLAY-BASEBALL) act out a key component of the sport, sometimes with an imaginary object. Other examples of body mime are DIG (with an imaginary shovel), PLAY-A-SLOT-MACHINE (putting a coin in an imaginary machine and pulling the lever) and DEAL CARDS (with an imaginary deck to imaginary players). Examples of hand mime using the nondominant hand as a base are

WRITE, RUBBER-STAMP, and RAKE.

Sign mime is commonly used in ASL discourse for actions which are easily imitated but for which there is no conventional sign in the lexicon. Sign mime can represent action sequences which would require the following English translations:

Lift up the hood of a car and look at the engine.

Remove a light bulb from its socket and replace it.

Put a pair of dice in a can, shake them, and pour them out.

Insert a videocassette in a videotape recorder and turn it on.

Reach for a billfold, remove a driver's license, and show it.

The freedom to resort to sign mime offers a great deal of latitude to speakers in ASL, especially in narratives. Often the speaker will simply re-live the experience for the benefit of the listener, acting out all over again what was said, what was done, with nonmanual cues supplying information as to how the agent(s) felt about the events as they transpired. The listener is treated to a dramatic re-enactment of the event, with sign mime carrying the major responsibility for the narration. Several examples of such a re-enactment of prior experiences can be observed in the videotape, *I Want to Talk.*

Infinitives

Some verbs do not complete a predicate by themselves, but require a complement. The complement may be a direct or indirect object. These are generally nouns or pronouns, not verbs. But there is one verb form that has some of the features of a noun, namely, the infinitive. Infinitives may serve as a complement for certain verbs, including WANT, LIKE, INTEND, TRY, PROMISE *etc.* Examples are as follows:

ME WANT GO

ME LIKE SWIM

ME INTEND STAY

WE TRY LEARN

In each of these examples, two verbs appear. The first is the main verb of the sentence; the second is its complementary infinitive.

Infinitive forms of verbs may also be used as a topic for a Topic/Comment sentence. In this role their substantive aspects are even more clear than in the preceding sentences. Examples are as follows:

TRAVEL ME DON'T-WANT

SWIM ME LIKE

STUDY ME SHOULD

The infinitive may be part of a substantive clause which serves as the topic for a comment or the object of a verb. Examples are as follows:

DRIVE WASHINGTON REQUIRE LONG TIME.

WORK IN FACTORY ALL DAY ME DON'T LIKE.

STAY IN HOSPITAL ME DON'T-WANT.

Infinitives are also used with modals, such as SHOULD, MUST, MIGHT, CAN, *etc.* Examples are as follows:

WE MUST WAIT.

WIND MIGHT CHANGE.

YOU CAN VISIT. These infinitives can be modified by adverbs, such as LONG-TIME, SHORT-TIME, TOMORROW, *etc.*

Infinitives can take an object. Examples are as follows:

WE MUST GO HOME.

YOU SHOULD STUDY SCIENCE.

ME WANT VISIT FRANCE.

HE PROMISE BUY TICKET.

SHE TRY FIND J-O-B.

Verb Inflections

There are several verb inflections in ASL which systematically affect the meaning of the verbs to which they are applied. There are some limitations to our knowledge about these constructions. A comprehensive and exhaustive list of ASL verb inflections has yet to be compiled. Secondly, limitations on the scope or generalizability of known inflections have yet to be examined fully. Finally, the labels that have been applied to them may fit some verbs better than others. Nevertheless, enough is known to warrant a treatment of some of the more frequently occurring inflections.

Durative

The *durative* inflection is a slow, elliptical, reduplicated execution. It implies that an action continues for a long period of time. This inflection may also be called *continuative*. Examples of verbs which may be inflected with a durative execution are FLY, DRIVE, WAIT, THINK, TALK, *etc.* When the nondominant hand provides a base for the sign, it is the nondominant hand that may execute the elliptical movement with the upper body participating as the dominant hand slowly and methodically executes the main action of the verb. Examples are WORK, PAY,

CLEAN, LEARN, READ *etc.* If a reduplicated execution is marked by an elliptical orbit but with no reduction in the speed of execution, the result may be the equivalent of the English progressive tenses. Thus, Mike Barry in *I Want to Talk* says of his progress in speech class, *I am learning [to talk]*. The verb, LEARN is reduplicated, and the nondominant had provides an elliptical orbit, but the execution is very fast. Thus, there is no implication that the learning process is slow or that it is taking a very long time, only that it is taking place during a period of time.

Iterative

The *iterative* inflection marks a verb as taking place repeatedly. It is characterized by a fast reduplication with brief junctures at the end of each repetition. Examples of verbs that lend themselves well to an iterative execution are GO, FLY, PAY, SUBSCRIBE, ANSWER, and SEND-A-LETTER. Alternatively, both hands may be used to imply a reiterated verb, as in ASK, TELL, LIE, EAT, INVITE, and TAKE-A-PILL.

Intensive

An *intensive* inflection marks a verb as involving a high level of emotional involvement or a great expenditure of effort. The execution is explosive, enlarged, and tense. The termination of the sign is forceful and abrupt. Examples of such explosive executions with a forceful stop are FINISH, PAY ATTENTION, FORGET, and TELL. Imperatives are very often executed with an intensive inflection, but declarative statements may also be intensive. If contact is involved in the execution, it is hard contact. Examples of contact signs that may be executed intensively are STOP, ACCEPT, WRITE-DOWN, and CANCEL. Perhaps out of self preservation, the intensive execution of body contact signs that are executed on the face or near the eyes deletes the body contact, coming to an abrupt stop near the point of contact as an alternative. Examples are THINK, KNOW, and EAT. More than one facial expression can accompany an intensive execution. For many intensives, including many imperatives, the brow is furrowed and the lips are pinched. An even more emphatic execution furrows the brow and holds the mouth open, as in THINK! or WHAT-FOR?!

Incremental and Incipient Action

The *incremental* inflection is an execution which is completed in stages. The initial execution is tentative, representing a sufficiently complete version to be recognized, but, at the same time, remaining clearly incomplete. If the execution is terminated at this point, the effect is to indicate the initiation of an action that was not completed, *i.e.*, an *incipient* action. Examples of meanings that can be communicated in this way are *I started to go, He meant to kill, we started to buy, She began to change, etc.* If the execution is completed in stages, the verb is then construed as incremental. For example, CHANGE can be executed in stages suggesting that the change took place a little at a time. One might translate, *She changed gradually,* or *She changed little by little.* Other verbs that can be executed with an incremental inflection are SUCCEED, GO, BEGIN, PROCEED, BRING, COME, SLEEP, APPROACH, and AWAKEN.

Complex Verb Forms

It should not be assumed that a verb can be inflected in only one way at a time or that, if the verb is inflected, it cannot be modified in some other way. For example, to translate the English sentence, *I kept handing out papers all night long,* one might execute GIVE with a durative inflection with spatial agreement with the imagined indirect objects. The sign sentence would be glossed ALL-NIGHT ME PAPER GIVE (1) GIVE (2) GIVE (3) GIVE (1) GIVE (2) GIVE (3) GIVE (1) GIVE (2) GIVE (3), where (1), (2) and (3) represent different locations associated with the indirect objects. By the same token, as long as the inflections are not mutually exclusive, they may be combined. An iterative and intensive execution can be superimposed, as in *I really kept telling him,* or an an iterative and an incipient execution can be combined, as in *I kept trying to start the car.* When it is considered that adverbs of manner may be incorporated with verbs that are already doubly inflected, it should be apparent that verbs may be modified in ASL in a variety of interesting and effective ways to communicate the desired meaning. Examples of complex English sentences that are likely to be translated by means of highly inflected executions with a great deal of incorporated meaning are the following:

I really don't want to have to spend four years paying off a new car.

ME PAY, PAY, PAY, PAY (durative inflection, intensive execution) FOUR YEARS FOR NEW CAR (juncture marker) ME DON'T-WANT (+ non-verbal negative).

I change the oil in my car regularly.

O-I-L, MY C-A-R, ME CHANGE CHANGE CHANGE (iterative, intensive) REGULARLY.

In the Fall you have to prune roses and cover them with dirt; then they will be safe until Spring.

R-O-S-E-S: FALL MUST CUT, CUT, CUT (reduplicated directional + eye gaze directed toward imaginary roses), DIRT

SCRAPE, SCRAPE, SCRAPE (directional), KEEP SAFE UNTIL SPRING.

Like the complexity of sentences, the complexity of verbs is limited only by the ingenuity of the speaker and the ability of the listener to understand what is said. Hearing people just beginning to learn ASL are likely to be greatly challenged by the opportunity to express their thoughts and feelings with such a highly inflected language as ASL. But native speakers of ASL seem to infer the speaker's intent without difficulty, even when the information seems to be coded with subtle non-manual cues.

Summary

Verbs are the key element of the predicate in sentences. They report what the subject is or does.

The tense of verbs is not marked by an inflection of the verb. Instead, a temporal frame of reference is established either by the situation or context or by explicit temporal adverbs, which usually precede the verb. Once a temporal frame of reference is established, it remains in force until changed. Temporal adverbs for the past (AGO), present (NOW) and future (WILL) may be modified so as to express the recent past, the immediate present, and the imminent future. They may also express the remote past and distant future. Other signs that are involved in the tense of verbs are FINISH, NOT-YET, and SINCE.

Many verbs can be executed directionally. For example, GIVE can begin in a location associated with the subject and proceed through space to a location associated with the indirect object. TELL can begin with the location for the subject and end at the location for the object. Directional agreement of verbs between subjects, objects, and indirect objects provides an important source of syntactic structure for ASL sentences. Verbs of motion in ASL must agree with any locatives that are involved in the discourse.

Since classifiers can describe the movement associated with nouns, they may function as verbs. Dual classifiers can indicate mutual action or interaction of subjects. Some verbs in the ASL lexicon (MEET, FOL-LOW, MARCH) may be derived from classifiers.

Infinitives often serve as the complement for verbs, occurring with verbs like WISH and WANT, and with modals, such as MUST, SHOULD, and CAN. Infinitives can be a part of a substantive clause which is the topic of a Topic/Comment sentence. Infinitives can be modified by adverbs, and some may take an object.

Verbs in ASL can be inflected so as to indicate an action that takes place over a period of time *(durative)*, an action that is repeated again and again *(iterative)*, an action that is begun and not completed *(incipient)* or that is carried out in stages *(incremental)*. Verbs are not limited to one inflection or one incorporated adverb per execution. Executions can become quite complex, conveying a great deal of information by the way in which the verb is executed and by means of nonmanual features that accompany the execution.

Chapter Six: Adverbs in American Sign Language

Definition

In spoken languages, an adverb is a word that modifies a verb, adjective, or another adverb. In sign languages adverbs may be signs (TRULY, ALWAYS, NEVER, VERY, ONCE, DAILY) or fingerspelled signs (E-A-R-L-Y, O-N-L-Y). They may also be incorporated in the manner of executing other signs. When adverbs are incorporated, there will be no specific sign that one can translate into English. The meaning will be included in the execution of the sign that incorporates the adverb.

Incorporation of Manner

Adverbs often play the role of indicating the *how* of an action. Many of these adverbs of manner end in the suffix -ly in English. Examples are *carefully, quickly, casually, laboriously, slowly, etc.* With rare exceptions, these adverbs are incorporated in the manner of executing a verb. Some verbs in English also imply something about manner. *Saunter* implies walking in a casual manner, and *stare* implies looking in a direct and prolonged manner. The ASL translations of these verbs would incorporate the implied manner in their executions. One can take a single verb in ASL, such as LOOK, and execute it in a large number of different ways, each one representing a different adverbial modifier. For example, one can LOOK-SUSPICIOUSLY, LOOK-LONGINGLY, LOOK-CONTEMPTUOUSLY, LOOK-INTERESTEDLY, LOOK-ANGRILY, LOOK-DISINTERESTEDLY, *etc.* Since it is virtually impossible to execute a verb in context devoid of manner, verbs typically connote some adverbial aspect even when it is not a salient part of the message. In a narrative about a prior event, the speaker will ordinarily reflect the same emotional states and the same attitudes or feelings that were experienced at the time of the event itself. Often it will be a judgment call whether a translation should attempt to do justice to all of the adverbial information that is included in such a narrative.

Since the incorporation of adverbs of manner is pervasive in ASL, attempts to sign English word for word often encounter difficulty. There are many adverbs in English for which ASL does not have a specific sign equivalent. English adverbs of manner are translatable into ASL, but not by means of specific signs. They are incorporated in the manner of executing the verb.

Very

The adverb VERY is generally included in sign lists as a part of the ASL lexicon. It appears to be an initialized version of MUCH. But this sign is used infrequently, principally because intensity is often incorporated in the execution of the adjective or adverb that *very* would modify. Thus, VERY-SLOWLY would be a modified version of SLOWLY, VERY-HARD a modified version of HARD, and VERY-BEAUTIFUL a modified version of BEAUTIFUL (Figure 19).

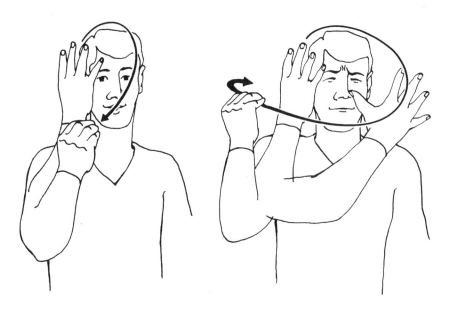

Fig. 19. Adjectives (BEAUTIFUL) can be modified to incorporate the adverb, VERY (VERY-BEAUTIFUL).

Color names are also intensified by a modified execution. For example, BLUE executed with a lateral movement is DEEP-BLUE. GREEN, YELLOW, and PURPLE are modified similarly. Nonmanual features also play a role. Intensified colors may be executed with squinted eyes, furrowed brows, and pinched lips. Such nonmanual features are especially important for DARK-RED, VERY-WHITE, and PITCH-BLACK.

The modification that adds intensity to an adjective or adverb is typically an embellished execution. It varies from sign to sign. The following are examples of the modification in execution that adds the notion of intensity:

BEAUTIFUL: Enlarge the circle into an ellipse and conclude the sign with clustered fingers making a circle and a full stop.

HARD: Execute forcefully with a high rebound from contact.

CLEAN: Execute slowly with furrowed brow and pinched lips; the breath may be sucked in.

TIRED: Change the tempo; begin slowly and end abruptly, with a forward body lean paralleling the execution.

GOOD: Increase the distance of the sign by elevating the dominant hand before its descent; make forceful contact.

SMALL, NARROW: Hunch shoulders, pinch lips, suck in breath, agitate the hands in their final positions.

WRONG: Begin slowly, end abruptly with a full stop near the chin; the initial position may begin with the hand turned outward so that the sign is executed with a twist of the wrist.

NEW: Increase the distance of the sign by starting farther off to the right and extending the movement after contact farther to the left.

HEAVY: Hunch the shoulders, furrow the brows, puff the cheeks.

COLD: Furrowed brows, pinched lips, tensed muscles.

BAD: Increase the distance of the sign by elevating the dominant hand after contact with the chin and then bring it forcefully downward.

EASY: Change the tempo; begin slowly and end abruptly; tilt the head back, squint the eyes, and avoid eye contact with the hands.

It is apparent that some features are shared by the intensified version of several of the above adjectives. Features that tend to be used rather frequently are a change in the temporal pattern of the execution (start slowly and end abruptly), an increase in the distance covered by the execution, additional muscle tension, and a facial expression which includes furrowed brows and pinched lips.

The role played by the furrowed brows and pinched lips deserves special comment. It may lead to some confusion on the part of those who are not native speakers of ASL, since such a facial expression is often perceived as hostile or aggressive, not the kind of face one would put on for BEAUTIFUL or WONDERFUL. Clearly, facial expressions in ASL are not merely *natural* expressions that are common to the human experience or pervasive in the larger culture or society. Facial expressions in ASL are rule-governed; they operate in a generalized fashion on a number of different linguistic elements, and they communicate information reliably among native speakers, information that would not be correctly interpreted by people who are outsiders to the language and its use.

In addition to the above, there are some general conditions that are likely to prevail during any intensive execution, including an incorporated *very*. The speaker is likely to establish or maintain eye contact with the listener. There may be a slight pause at the beginning of the sign that is to be intensified, preparing the listener for the emphasis. Following the execution, eye contact may be sustained so as to verify from the listener's reaction that the emphasis was communicated. If a part of the emphasis involved a deliberate gaze off into the distance (an option for EASY, SLOWLY, FAR, and some other adverbs), direct eye contact with the listener may be resumed at the conclusion of the execution.

Temporal Adverbs

Temporal adverbs establish the time in which an action took place. They are often implicated in establishing the tense of verbs in ASL. For example, if a sentence begins with the adverb YESTERDAY, one would expect the verb of that sentence to be in the past tense. If it began with TOMORROW, one would expect the verb to be in the future. Not surprisingly, these adverbs (and others) are marked by the same spatial distinction that marks other adverbs which establish a temporal frame of reference for a narrative or discourse, namely, a backward movement for PAST or AGO and a forward movement for FUTURE or WILL. Thus, TOMORROW moves forward along the cheek, and YESTERDAY moves backward along the cheek (A regional variant moves from cheek to shoulder).

Other adverbs which involve forward movements for the future and backward movements for the past are the highly inflected forms of WEEK and YEAR. With only the temporal aspect included in the execution, we have NEXT-WEEK, LAST-WEEK, NEXT-YEAR and LAST-YEAR. It should be mentioned that there is an idiomatic execution of LAST-YEAR that wiggles the raised right index finger, thumb extended, back toward the right shoulder. An example of this idiomatic usage can be found in *I Want to Talk*, (p. 55). With number as well as temporal aspect included in the execution, we have the following:

TWO-WEEKS-FROM-NOW (Figure 20)
THREE-WEEKS-FROM-NOW
FOUR-WEEKS-FROM-NOW
TWO-YEARS-FROM-NOW
THREE-YEARS-FROM-NOW
FOUR-YEARS-FROM-NOW
TWO-WEEKS-AGO
THREE-WEEKS-AGO
FOUR-WEEKS-AGO
TWO-YEARS-AGO
THREE-YEARS-AGO
FOUR-YEARS-AGO

Fig. 20. TWO-WEEKS-FROM-NOW incorporates number and tense in the execution of WEEK.

The executions for MONTH differ somewhat from WEEK and YEAR. NEXT-MONTH can be indicated by moving both hands forward in an arc as the sign is executed. LAST-MONTH requires an arc extending somewhat back toward the right shoulder. Numbers may be incorporated in these execution as in TWO-MONTHS, THREE-MONTHS, FOUR-MONTHS, TWO-MONTHS-FROM-NOW, TWO-MONTHS-AGO, *etc.* There are also idiomatic executions for TWO-DAYS-AGO,

TWO-DAYS-FROM-NOW, THREE-DAYS-AGO, THREE-DAYS-FROM-NOW, A-FEW-DAYS-AGO, A-FEW-DAYS-FROM-NOW.

Temporal adverbs implying regularity are typically represented by a reduplicated execution. The following are examples:

TOMORROW (reduplicated = DAILY)
WEEK (reduplicated = WEEKLY)
NEXT-YEAR (reduplicated = YEARLY)
MONTH (reduplicated = MONTHLY)
ONCE (reduplicated = SOMETIMES)
AGAIN (reduplicated = OFTEN)
NEXT(?) (reduplicated = OCCASIONALLY)
RIGHT(?) (reduplicated = REGULARLY)

Two of the above, OCCASIONALLY, and REGULARLY also involve a movement in space as the signs are executed, and SOMETIMES involves a slow, elliptical reduplication. The root or base for the two signs, NEXT and RIGHT, are followed by a question mark, indicating that the relationship between the single and reduplicated executions is uncertain.

Signs for times of the day typically represent the horizon with the horizontal left arm, and the right arm represents the position of the sun. Thus, MORNING brings the right forearm up from under the left arm, while AFTERNOON slants the right arm outward across the left arm. Other positions that can be depicted by this strategy are NOON and MIDNIGHT. If the right arm is deliberately moved through a portion of the appropriate space, one can express the meanings ALL-MORNING, ALL-AFTERNOON, ALL-DAY, or ALL-NIGHT.

A special inflection is available for indicating a recurring event. It involves a vertical movement for days of the week and a horizontal movement for times of the day. Thus, FRIDAY, is a circled "F" hand, and FRIDAYS or EVERY-FRIDAY is a downward movement of the "F" hand. An alternate execution moves the "F" hand downward in a series of small arcs. A more specific recurring event can be specified; for example, EVERY-OTHER-FRIDAY may be indicated by moving the "F" hand downward in a series of long arcs. Similarly, MORNING is executed by raising the right forearm under the horizontal left arm, and MORN-INGS or EVERY-MORNING moves the entire configuration laterally in neutral space. NIGHTS or AT NIGHT involves a lateral movement of the execution, NIGHT.

Negatives

Negatives are often adverbs. Signs that negate verbs include NOT, NOTHING, NOT-YET, and NEVER. There is a prohibitive sign, DON'T, that is often an imperative verb, but is sometimes used as an emphatic negative adverb. Some verbs imply a negation without a headshake or an explicit sign for the negative, *e.g.*, CAN'T, WON'T. In English these are contractions from *can not* and *will not*. In ASL they are lexical items which include the negation as a part of the meaning. They could also be glossed UNABLE or REFUSE.

A special comment is in order on the use of NOTHING as an adverb. It is not always an adverb. It can be a predicate nominative, as in HE SAY NOTHING. As an adverb it may come last in a sentence, negating the verb. For example, ME GET LETTER FROM HOME NOTHING would be translated, *I didn't get a single letter from home.* NOTHING may also be used as a negative answer to Yes/No questions. For example, LIBRARY, SHE GO? might be answered NOTHING SHE, meaning *She did not.*

A very small number of verbs incorporate negation in the manner of their execution. The movement that implies the negative is a turning away of the hands from the face or body. Thus, WANT may be negated as DON'T-WANT, KNOW can be negated as DON'T-KNOW, and LIKE can be negated as DON'T-LIKE.

It is common for a headshake to accompany a negative, whether signed or incorporated. Thus, a headshake is likely to accompany the execution of NOT, NEVER, NOT-YET, and CAN'T. Alteratively, the head may simply be turned aside and gaze averted for WON'T, DON'T-LIKE, DON'T-WANT, DON'T-KNOW, and NOTHING.

Since a headshake is, itself, a negation, it can be used in the absence of a specific sign to negate a verb. Thus, ME GO executed with a headshake accompanying the verb would be translated *I am not going* or *I did not go.* By the same token, a nod of the head accompanying a verb adds a touch of emphasis. ME GO executed with a head nod accompanying the verb would be translated, *I really am going,* or *I really did go.*

Adverbial Numerals

Ordinal numerals are sometimes used as adverbs to mark enumerate points, as in FIRSTLY, SECONDLY, THIRDLY, *etc.* A common ASL strategy is to strike the right index finger against the ball of the left thumb for FIRSTLY. (Left-handed persons may use the left hand as the dominant hand.) SECONDLY is signed by extending the left thumb and index finger, representing the numeral 2, and touching the right index fingertip to the left index fingertip. THIRDLY presents a 3 on the left hand and touches the right index fingertip to the tip of the left middle finger. For FOURTHLY and FIFTHLY the right index fingertip is touched to the tip of the little finger of the left hand as it presents the numerals 4 and 5, respectively. LASTLY, FINALLY strikes the tip of the right little finger against the tip of the extended left little finger with a downward movement of the right hand. An alternate version executes the sign with the right index finger.

Ordinal numerals may also be executed with the right hand making a hook in neutral space, making contact with the left palm, or making a lateral movement toward the right in neutral space. These executions may be used both for ordinal adverbs and for ordinal adjectives.

Locatives

Although there is an explicit sign, HERE, that is used as an adverb of place (both hands, palms up, are circled in neutral space in front of the body), HERE may also be indicated by pointing downward with the index finger. A more distant location is always referenced by means of an index, *i.e.*, a pointed index finger. If the distant location is very far away, the index may be executed in an arc, as if it had to hurdle intervening lands and buildings to identify the location. When a location is not to be specified so distinctly, the dominant hand, palm down, may execute a tight circle near the body for AROUND HERE or some distance away from the body for AROUND-THERE, IN-THAT-VICINITY. Thus, ASL has both a specific index (HERE, THERE) executed with the pointed index finger and a general index (AREA, VICINITY) executed with the palm (Figure 21). The spatial nature of ASL allows AREA to be executed in any plane, vertically if the reference is to a vertical surface, such as a wall or fence, diagonally if the reference is to a slanting surface, such as the slope of a hill.

Locatives may be incorporated in the directional execution of verbs. Thus, GO may sometimes be glossed GO-THERE. The same can be said of DRIVE, WALK, and FLY. Meanwhile, the execution of classifiers often includes information about the location or spatial arrangement Thus, there are a variety of strategies in ASL for specifying location or direction.

Adverbial Phrases

Prepositional phrases occur very frequently in ASL, and many of them are adverbial phrases. Examples of adverbial prepositional phrases are ME LIVE IN O-H-I-O, ME WORK WITH BROTHER, ME GET LETTER FROM MOTHER. The preposition may be understood, as in ME LIVE WASHINGTON, ME DRIVE NEW-YORK.

Prepositions typically use the nondominant hand to establish a reference point, and the meaning of the preposition is conveyed by the relationship or the movement of the dominant hand relative to the nondominant hand. For example, TO and FROM both use the extended index finger of the nondominant hand as the reference, and TO points

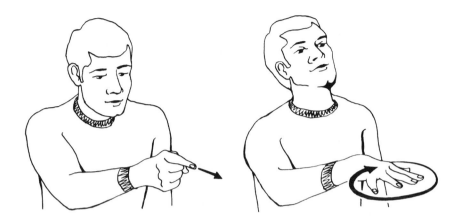

Fig. 21. A locative index can be specific (THERE) or general (AROUND-THERE).

the index finger of the dominant hand to the other index finger tip, and FROM draws the dominant "X" hand back from the nondominant hand's index finger. IN and OUT also use the nondominant hand to present an opening relative to which the clustered fingertips of the dominant hand can enter or emerge. OVER and UNDER are executed relative to the nondominant hand, palm down, THROUGH passes the dominant hand between the third and fourth fingers of the nondominant hand, BETWEEN places the dominant hand between the thumb and index finger of the nondominant hand, and WITH places the two fists, thumbs up, side by side in neutral space. There are exceptions, of course. WITHOUT is a compound of WITH + OPEN-HANDS. The execution sometimes resembles a negative incorporation. FOR is still signed as it was 200 years ago by the Abbe de l'Epee to translate the French *pour;* the extended index finger is touched to the forehead and then turned outward with a twist of the wrist.

Adverbial Clauses

Adverbial clauses provided information as to time, place, or manner. The relative adverbs introducing these clauses are WHEN, WHERE, and HOW. Examples of such adverbial clauses are

ME SUCCEED WHEN ME TRY HARD.

ME TRAVEL WHERE CAN FIND INTERESTING SEE THERE THERE.

ME EXPLAIN HOW MAKE BREAD.

The clause is sometimes left understood, as when Mike Barry explained that his sister was too young to know the rules of various games. He said, ME TELL TELL HOW [TO PLAY] (see *I Want to Talk*, p. 22).

Summary

An adverb in English is a word that modifies a verb, adjective, or another adverb. This definition can also serve for ASL, because there are adverbial modifiers in ASL. But adverbs are often expressed nonmanually, as in verbs which incorporate adverbs of manner in their execution, or when VERY is incorporated in the execution of an adverb or adjective rather than signed. Both manual and nonmanual features play a role in the incorporation of manner and the incorporation of VERY. The manual executions are often modified in rule-governed ways which involve changes in the rhythm and tempo of the execution, changes in the size of the sign or the vigor with which it is executed, reduplication, an added flourish on the end of the execution, or other inflections. Meanwhile, nonmanual features generally also play an important role, especially the facial expression and body attitude.

Temporal adverbs are important for establishing the the tense of verbs in ASL narratives and discourse. Properly placed temporal adverbs enable the listener to interpret correctly the temporal frame of reference. Some temporal adverbs are highly inflected, especially those that are used frequently to refer to the past and future. Among the signs that may be inflected for tense and number are TOMORROW, YESTERDAY, WEEK, MONTH, and YEAR. One can also distinguish between the recent and remote past and between the imminent and remote future.

Negative adverbs include NOT, NOTHING, NOT-YET, and NEVER. Negatives may also be incorporated in the execution of a small number of verbs, or they may be indicated nonmanually by a shake of the head.

Ordinal numerals may also be used adverbially. There are a variety of manual signs in ASL for ordinal numerals. Some present the numeral on the nondominant hand and index it with the dominant hand, while others use the dominant hand to execute the numeral with a hook, a lateral movement, or in contact with the other palm.

Locatives are generally expressed by means of a specific index (a pointed index finger) or a general index (a circled palm). These may reference locations near the speaker or remote from the speaker. Locatives are often incorporated in the execution of verbs or classifiers.

Phrases and clauses may also function as adverbial modifiers. Prepositional phrases are composed of a preposition and its object. Adverbial clauses are typically introduced by a relative adverb, such as HOW, WHEN, WHERE, and WHY. Adverbs that modify verbs and other adverbs are part of the predicate of a sentence. Adverbs that modify adjectives are part of the subject when they modify adjectives associated with the subject of the sentence and part of the predicate when they modify adjectives that are associated with the object of the verb.

Chapter Seven: Adjectives in American Sign Language

Definitions

An adjective is a manual or nonmanual feature which modifies a noun. Adjectives may be descriptive (HOT, BIG, HEAVY) or definitive (TWO, EACH, NONE). Adjectives may be specific signs, often sharing a very similar field of meaning with the English word that they translate *e.g.*, STRONG, NEW, or BEAUTIFUL, Adjectives may also be executed as graphic depictions, similar (but not identical) to drawing in the air. Specific handshapes and movements may serve as size and shape specifiers, such as SMALL-ROUND-OBJECT (like a coin), LARGE-ROUND-OBJECT (like a pancake), RECTANGULAR-OBJECT (like an index card), or LARGE-CYLINDRICAL-OBJECT (like a gasoline storage tank). Signs for objects that manifest a certain size and shape may be a product of such size and shape specifiers, *e.g.*, GLASS and FACE. Adjectives may also be incorporated in the manner of executing nouns, *e.g.*, a BIG-HOUSE may be signed with an enlarged execution, a BIG-PLANE may be signed with puffed cheeks, squinted eyes, and a slowed execution, and a HEAVY-BALL may be signed by holding an imaginary ball with a great deal of effort. Appropriate nonmanual signals are often presented simultaneously with the execution of adjectives like TIRED, ANGRY, and DISAPPOINTED. Nonmanual features of ASL may serve an adjectival function in their own right, as when puffed cheeks imply that an object is HEAVY or BIG and when air sucked in through narrowed lips imply that an object is THIN or SMALL. Thus, adjectives may take the form of specific signs, graphic depictions, or size and shape specifiers, or they may be incorporated in the manner of executing a noun. They may be accompanied by nonmanual signals, or a nonmanual execution can imply a descriptive adjective, *e.g.*, HEAVY or THIN.

Derivations

Adjectives are derived from a wide variety of sources, just as are nouns. Some seem to be highly motivated (STRONG, COLD, BIG, SOFT, OLD); others would be almost impossible to interpret without prior knowledge of their meaning (NEW, WRONG, FANCY, YELLOW). Motivated adjectives must be selected with some care. The adjective *hot* is signed differently for *hot stove* and *hot summer*. A very different execution would be required to translate *big house* and *big diamond*.

Some adjectives are formed by compounding. RICH is derived from MONEY and HEAP. WET is derived from WATER and SQUEEZE. NOISY is derived from HEAR and QUAKE. Adjectives executed with the middle finger tip playing a prominent role often have to do with feeling, *e.g.*, SICK, THRILLED, DEPRESSED, EXCITED, and SHARP. Some adjectives may be derived from classifiers, *e.g.*, UNDECIDED (legs straddling a fence). A few adjectives are initialized (BLUE, PURE), but this strategy for generating signs seems to have been used much more for nouns than for adjectives. In general, adjectives reflect considerable variability in their derivations, and they illustrate the productivity of ASL, that is, its ability as a language to permit signs to be developed for which the deaf community has a need.

Noun/Adjective Sequence

When an adjective modifies a noun in ASL, it often follows the noun that it modifies, *e.g.*, HE HAVE HOUSE NICE, ME WANT CAR NEW. The opposite sequence is permitted (HE HAVE NICE HOUSE), but it seems to make sense in a visual language first to specify the noun and then to add the descriptors. The sequence, adjective/noun, may be an influence from English.

There are exceptions to the rule that adjectives may follow or precede the noun that they modify. When a noun is used as an adjective, as in BIRD CAGE, BABY DOLL, BABY BUGGY, DOLL HOUSE, *etc.*, the adjective always comes first before the noun. A second exception has to do with the noun TIME. The sequence TWO TIME is construed as *two times* in English, but the sequence TIME TWO is construed as *two o'clock*.

Antonyms

A large set of adjective signs have antonyms. Some of them can be considered synonym/antonym pairs, since the form of antonym is in some way the opposite of the synonym. Examples are BIG and SMALL, TALL and SHORT, SAME and DIFFERENT. Others are more or less motivated by their meaning, with the result that their executions make sense in relation to each other. Examples of such pairs are MANY and

FEW, FAT and THIN, TRUE and FALSE, SOFT and HARD, NOISY and QUIET, LIGHT and DARK. Still others are relatively arbitrary. At least it would be hard to guess the meaning of either member of the pair without prior knowledge, and the relationship between the synonym and antonym is purely semantic, not structural. Examples of such signs are RIGHT and WRONG, SHORT TIME and LONG TIME. An examination of a large number of synonym antonym pairs in ASL suggests that there is no single strategy that can be cited as providing a basis for generating antonyms. Although some of them are structurally opposite, others are simply motivated in their own right, and still others are relatively arbitrary. Nevertheless, for any descriptive adjectives that can be imagined to have an opposite meaning, ASL undoubtedly has a way to represent it.

Predicate Adjectives

Not all adjectives modify the noun that they describe. When the verb is an implied copula, such as *is, am, are, were, etc.,* in English, an adjective may be a part of the predicate. The construction is similar to a predicate nominative. Both are known as *complements,* because they complete the meaning of a verb. When the subject is a pronoun, it is often repeated after the predicate adjective or predicate nominative. This seems to be especially true when the pronoun is an INDEX. Examples of predicate adjectives follow:

INDEX-HE STRONG INDEX-HE.

INDEX-THEY HAPPY INDEX-THEY.

INDEX-ME SORRY INDEX-ME.

INDEX-HE FAMOUS INDEX-HE.

INDEX-SHE EXPERT INDEX-SHE.

Predicate adjectives also occur after the verbs SEEM, LOOK, BECOME, TASTE, FEEL, SMELL, I. etc. Examples follow:

INDEX-ME FEEL FINE.

INDEX-HE LOOK SICK.

INDEX-THAT TASTE LOUSY.

INDEX-HE SEEM TIRED.

INDEX-THEY BECOME ANGRY.

Graphic Depictions

Graphic depictions, like sign mime, require cautious treatment in a discussion of ASL grammar. They do not seem to be subject to syntactic rules. But it is not the case that *anything goes.* There are phonological rules that govern what is and what is not permissible, and the execution will generally be confined to the ASL *Sign Space*. It may be that these rules have more to do with what the eye can see and what the body can do than with any specific set of linguistic principles. But if speech is specifically tuned to the human ear, why should not ASL accommodate the human eye? In any case, graphic depictions afford an opportunity to be somewhat original and creative, since the speaker may use hands and body to build an image in three-dimensional space that the listener can construct in his or her mind.

Examples of graphic depiction are hard to gloss into English words, since they are based on the rules of pictorial composition rather than verbal sequences. The signs HOUSE, WINDOW, and TOWER (the latter a size, shape specifier) may be signed in various positions to depict an ornate Victorian mansion with many windows and gables and a huge tower on one corner. Fingers and hands may trim the house with the usual gingerbread to complete the effect. Proposed improvements to a deaf club can be depicted by showing an extended roof at the back of the building with a barbecue on one side (represented by sign mime manipulating skewers of meat), fence posts (classifiers) surrounding the property supporting a decorative chain fence (size and shape specifiers), a curved driveway (directional execution) leading from the street to the front of the building with several pairs of lights on both sides of the driveway spaced at equal intervals to the street.

Graphic depiction is often combined with sign mime to create a blend of drama and description vivid in detail both for action and for visual information. As a matter of fact, experienced teachers of ASL may discover that art students and theatre majors seem to have a relative advantage in discovering the strategies for making ASL lively and interesting as a language. Nonverbal exercises involving picture descriptions and dramatic enactments may serve as introductions for students of all types of backgrounds to some of the unique and powerful strategies that are available in ASL for communicating information visually.

Definitive Adjectives

There are two types of definitive adjectives, numeral adjectives (TWO BOOK, SECOND PLACE) and pronouns used as adjectives (THAT BOOK, EVERY STUDENT). Since numerals and pronouns in adjectival positions are governed by grammatical rules, a brief discussion is warranted.

Cardinal Numerals Used as Adjectives

Cardinal numerals can be executed on one hand in ASL. Any cardinal numeral can be used as an adjective. The numerals 1, 2, 3, 4, and 5 are executed by using the index finger, index and middle fingers, thumb, index, and middle fingers, four fingers, and all five fingers, respectively. The numerals 6, 7, 8, and 9 involve contact with the thumb tip by the little, fourth, middle, and index fingers, respectively. For 10 the raised thumb is wiggled. The numerals 11, 12, 13, 14, and 15 flick the appropriate fingers outward from a closed position or wiggle the appropriate finger in place with the hand turned toward the body. For 16, 17, 18, and 19 the hand is twisted at the wrist so as to present outward the numerals 6, 7, 8, and 9. The numeral 20 taps the thumb and index finger tips together. The numerals 21, 22, 23, and 25 are irregular. For 21, the thumb is wiggled as the index finger is extended. For 22 the numeral 2 is presented twice with a small movement to the right. For 23 the middle finger is wigged as the 3 hand is presented. For 25 the middle finger is wiggled as the 5 hand is presented. All other numerals up to 99 are regular, that is, two numerals are presented with a slight movement to the right, the first giving the numeral at the tens place and the second at the unit place, *e.g.*, THREE FIVE for *thirty-five* and SIX TWO for *sixty-two*. The numeral 100 is ONE C, probably borrowed from the Roman numeral. The numeral 1000 is ONE M, with the M signed in contact with the left palm. Given these basic forms, any numeral can be constructed. For example, TWO M SIX C FIVE THREE is 2,653. Examples of cardinal numerals used as adjectives follow:

ME HAVE CAR TWO.

ME BUY SIX BOOK.

WANT PLAY-CARDS? NEED PEOPLE FOUR.

Fractions are represented by signing the numerator first and then, below it, the denominator. Thus, THREE FOUR, with FOUR signed lower than THREE in space, would be *three fourths*. Compound fractions present the numeral first and then the fraction slightly to the right. THREE ONE HALF properly located in space would be interpreted *three and one half*.

Calendar years are signed as they are spoken in English. Thus, 1985 would be signed NINETEEN EIGHTY FIVE.

Ordinal Numerals Used as Adjectives

Ordinal numerals may also be used as adjectives (MY FIRST TIME VISIT WASHINGTON, ME DRINK SECOND CUP COFFEE). There are at least two sets of ordinal adjectives. One hooks the numeral in space in front of the shoulder. A regional variant draws the numeral horizontally from left to right in neutral space (right to left for left-handed persons). The other set of ordinal adjectives involves both hands. The nondominant hand presents the numeral, and the index finger of the dominant hand touches the fingertip of the last relevant finger of the numeral.

Cardinal adjectives often follow the noun that they modify (ME HAVE CHILDREN THREE), but they may precede the noun (ME HAVE TWO GIRL ONE BOY). Ordinal numerals generally precede the noun that they modify, but they may be repeated again after the noun (MY SECOND BOY, SECOND, NOW LIVE CALIFORNIA).

Once the nondominant hand is implicated in establishing an ordinal sequence, the fingers of the nondominant hand that served to indicate which noun was in which position may subsequently be used pronominally to reference those nouns. In the following example, the thumb is used for the first child, the index finger for the second, and so on down to the little finger for the fifth. Then the fingers are used over again in pairs to reference the fourth and second child and the third and first child.

ME HAVE FIVE CHILDREN. FIRST GIRL, SECOND BOY, THIRD BOY, FOURTH GIRL, FIFTH BOY. FOURTH SECOND HEARING, THIRD FIRST DEAF, FIFTH DON'T KNOW, STILL BABY.

This would be translated into English as follows:

I have five children. The first was a girl, the second a boy, the third a boy, the fourth a girl, and the fifth a boy. The fourth and second children are hearing. The third and first are deaf. The fifth we don't know. He is still a baby.

There are other adjectives of number or amount less specific than cardinal adjectives. Examples are MANY, SOME, FEW.

Pronouns Used as Adjectives

The second type of definitive adjective is a pronoun used as an adjective. Examples are THESE PAPERS and EVERY HOUSE. The sequence may be either noun/pronoun or pronoun/noun. It is permissible to say ME NEED PAPERS THOSE, or THEY TAX HOUSE EVERY. Interrogative pronouns may also be used as an adjectives (WHAT TIME YOU LEAVE?).

Articles

Adjectival functions spelled out in English by means of articles *a, an, the* are often understood in ASL. For example, in the sentence TRAIN LATE, a definite adjective (the article *the)* is understood. It is not likely that the speaker is saying *A train is late*. On the other hand, if a train stops, and someone asks WHY?, the answer MAN GET-OFF implies an indefinite article, *A man got off*, since no particular man is implicated. In English it is generally ungrammatical to have a noun occur without an article. In ASL the article is generally understood.

Comparison of Adjectives

The adjective most frequently executed with comparative and superlative forms is GOOD, BETTER, BEST. The comparative form omits the downward movement of the dominant hand toward the other palm and, instead, raises the thumb of the dominant hand upward near the shoulder. A higher elevation of the thumb implies the superlative, BEST. It would appear that the same approach could supply comparative and superlative forms to other adjectives, *e.g.*, CLEAN, CLEANER, CLEANEST, and HOT, HOTTER, HOTTEST. This is one option, but not the most frequent strategy for intensifying an adjective. Ordinarily the comparative form of adjectives is incorporated in the manner of execution. For example, HOT is executed with a neutral facial expression with a movement similar to the citation form. HOTTER may be executed with a forward body lean, squinted eyes, and a slightly more emphatic execution. HOTTEST intensifies the nonmanual features and adds more force and distance to the execution. Spatial organization of the nouns that are to be compared may also be involved in the comparison of adjectives in ASL. If HOT is indexed left to provide a basis for comparison, VERY-HOT indexed right is HOTTER. Thus, although the thumbs up sign (generally glossed CHIEF) can imply a more intensive form of the adjective, the manner of execution is the more common strategy for representing intensive forms with nonmanual features and spatial organization playing an important role.

There is another sign commonly used to compare an adjective with a base or standard. This is the sign LITTLE-BIT. Thus, CAR LITTLE-BIT BIG is a car that is not as big as the biggest car around, but it is bigger than the average. Similarly, HOUSE LITTLE-BIT SMALL is not the smallest in the world, but it is smaller than the one previously referenced or smaller than the average house. Viewed in this light, LITTLE-BIT can be considered a sign that may be used to mark comparative forms of adjectives.

The thumbs up sign CHIEF can occur alone. When it stands as a predicate adjective, it simply means that the subject is eminent or outstanding in some way. When it modifies a verb, it is usually glossed CHIEFLY, MOSTLY, as in MOSTLY ME LIKE GAMBLING. When it modifies an adjective, it may be construed as a comparative, even when the adjective is understood. For example, if the first speaker says MY

TEACHER STRICT, the second speaker may reply MY TEACHER CHIEF The English translation would be, (Speaker 1): *My teacher is strict.* (Speaker 2): *My teacher is more strict.*

Incorporated Adjectives

Adjectives can also be incorporated in the manner of executing the noun. BIG-HOUSE can be represented by an enlarged execution that implies a house that is larger than average. CURVED-DRIVEWAY can be represented by executing the sign ROAD with a long, smooth curve. DILAPIDATED-HOUSE can be executed by tilting the sign HOUSE to the side as if it were about to collapse.

Nonmanual features may supply an adjective to a noun that is executed simultaneously. Thus, PLANE executed with puffed cheeks implies HUGE-PLANE, and CAR executed with puffed cheeks implies BIG-CAR, as in Figure 22. The nonmanual execution, puffed cheeks, a generalizable inflection for quantity or weight. The same nonmanual adjective may imply HEAVY-DRAPES, BIG-BOX, HEAVY-BUCKET, *etc.* The opposite, THIN-DRAPES, TINY-BOX, FLIMSY-BUCKET can be indicated nonmanually by pursing the lips and drawing in breath. The eyes are usually squinted as well.

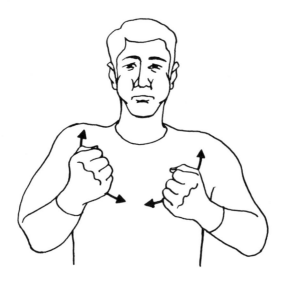

Fig. 22. The sign CAR can be executed with nonmanual features, such as puffed cheeks, to incorporate the adjective, BIG.

Puffed cheeks and sucked-in breath are not the only nonmanual adjective that can be applied to a noun. One can imply nonmanually that there is a SMELLY-FISH, a BORING-LECTURE, a SCARY-MOVIE, *etc.* Thus, adjectives in ASL do not need a specific sign for them to be represented in the discourse. They may be incorporated in the manner of executing the noun or they can be signaled by nonmanual features that accompany the execution of the noun.

Even nonmanual features of ASL that accompany a verb can have adjectival significance. Thus, when BALL is the subject, a labored execution of the verb THROW can imply that the BALL is HEAVY. The sentence, ME THROW (labored) BALL can only be translated as *I threw a heavy ball* Even sign mime can imply adjectives in the execution. A sign mime execution for REEL-IN-A-FISH can imply that the fish is struggling, that it is heavy, or that it is easy to land by the way in which the sign mime is executed. A sign mime of SHOVEL-SNOW can imply how deep the snow is or how hard it is to shovel it.

A special form of incorporation is the idiomatic execution of small amounts of money (below $10.00). A deeply hooked numeral, *e.g.*, SIX (hooked downward in neutral space) is the sign SIX-DOLLARS. Cents may be added, *e.g.*, EIGHT (hooked) SEVEN FIVE (with the FIVE slightly to the right) is $8.75.

Adjectives of size and quantity

There are a variety of strategies in ASL for describing the size, number, or amount of something. One of these is size/shape specifiers. They are used very frequently in ASL; consequently, they will be treated first. Sometimes this strategy may be used to refer to the item, itself, namely, by indicating its size and shape. In that case, the result would be a substantive (a noun or pronoun). Some authorities include size and shape specifiers as a type of classifier. Once the noun to which the size/shape specifier refers has been identified, the size/shape specifier, like a classifier, can indicate where the noun is located. For example, a handful of nuts on the surface of a table can be indicated by signing NUTS and then specifying how they are scattered about or arranged on a flat surface by means of a size/shape specifier, *e.g.*, a circle formed by the thumb and index finger. Similarly, when a larger circle formed by the thumb and index finger of both hands is moved from one location to another around a table, the result is to indicate the location of several round, thin objects, *e.g.*, dinner plates. Thus, size/shape specifiers sometimes specify more than size and shape. Nevertheless, size and shape specifiers will be treated here as descriptive adjectives.

Size and Shape Specifiers

Size and shape specifiers using the thumb and index fingers of both hands may trace the outline of various rectangular objects, such as RULER, LICENSE, CHECK, CHARGE-CARD, POST-CARD, *etc.* Round objects that are small can be distinguished from round objects that are large (Figure 23). Curved thumbs and index fingers may be used to specify the size and shape of ASH-TRAY, SAUCER, PLATE, PLATTER, or TABLE-TOP. The index finger and thumb of the dominant hand may form a circle to represent the size and shape of a coin, token, or medallion. For irregular shapes, one can draw in the air with the index finger of the dominant hand. If the shape is irregular but symmetrical, both index fingers can be used.

Fig. 23. Size and shape specifiers distinguish small round objects from large round objects.

Size and shape specifiers are used freely in ASL to provide descriptive information. Often the noun is specified first, and the size and shape specifiers follow. Thus MIRROR may be followed by a symmetrical sign using both hands with curved thumbs and index fingers to indicate BIG-AND-ROUND. Alternately, the index fingers of both hands could trace a BIG-SQUARE, SMALL-SQUARE, BIG-VERTICAL-RECTANGLE, SMALL-HORIZONTAL-RECTANGLE, *etc.* If a size and shape specifier is used without a designated noun, it may be construed as a classifier. For example, someone seated at a table might ask WHERE MY [SIZE/SHAPE SPECIFIER FOR PLATE]? The size/shape specifier that would be used in this sentence is sometimes found in published lists of signs as part of the ASL lexicon.

Mass Quantifiers

Mass nouns are a special class of nouns characterized by the fact that one cannot count how many of them there are. Examples are WATER, CHEESE, MONEY, *etc.* There are adjectives that are particularly suited to modify mass nouns, inasmuch as they specify, relatively speaking, how much of the noun is indicated. Thus ME WANT LITTLE-BIT WATER says something else than ME WANT SOME WATER or ME WANT MUCH WATER. Adjectives modifying mass nouns may precede or follow the noun that they modify. Both ME HAVE ENOUGH MONEY and ME HAVE MONEY ENOUGH are acceptable in ASL. Size and shape specifiers can also be used to quantify mass nouns, *e.g.,* by showing how much of a drink should be poured in a glass.

Count nouns exist in some specific number. Adjectives that can modify count nouns include cardinal and ordinal numerals and the signs MANY, SEVERAL, and FEW. The signs for these adjectives are derived from the presentation of the fingers of one or both hands. In the case of MANY, SEVERAL and FEW, when the fingers are presented all at once, the sign is MANY. When the fingers of only one hand are presented very slowly, the sign is FEW. SEVERAL lies midway between these executions. Like the cardinal numerals, these signs may precede or follow the nouns that they modify. VERY-MANY can be executed with nonmanual features presented along with the sign: a slowed execution, hunched shoulders, puffed cheeks, squinted eyes, tensed muscles. The clenched fists may be agitated in alternating movements before the sign MANY is executed. VERY-FEW can be executed with nonmanual features presented with the sign: slowed execution, hunched shoulders, sucked in breath, squinted eyes. The hands may be held close to the face and the eyes squinted for the execution of VERY-FEW.

Negative Adjectives

The two "O" hands are drawn apart horizontally for the pronoun, NONE, and the adjective NO. Examples of the adjectival use of the sign are ME HAVE NO MONEY, CAR HAVE NO GAS, *etc.* The adjective may follow the noun, *e.g.,* ME HAVE MONEY NONE. An alternative sign presents the numeral ZERO, the right "O" hand, as in ME HAVE MONEY ZERO.

Summary

Adjectives are elements in a sentence that modify nouns. There are descriptive adjectives and definitive adjectives. Descriptive adjectives provide information about the appearance of the quality of the nouns that they modify. Definitive adjectives tell us how many nouns are specified, or whether the specification is specific or indefinite.

Adjectives, like nouns, are derived from a variety of sources. Some are iconic. Others are not. Many adjectives have antonyms in ASL. Some of them constitute synonym/antonym pairs; others are not related to each other. In ASL sentences, the adjective will often follow the noun that it modifies. Exceptions are nouns used as adjectives and numerals referring to clock time.

Definitive adjectives include numerals and pronouns. Since numerals are used very frequently, there are many irregular forms. Articles, common in English, are not used in ASL to distinguish definite from indefinite references to a noun. The situation and context are sufficient to remove any ambiguity.

Adjectives can be compared as to degree by means of a thumbs up sign which functions very much like the English suffixes *-er* and *-est*. In addition, the sign LITTLE-BIT can provide information about an adjective relative to some standard. Finally, an index to a standard followed by an index to a more intensive execution provides a strategy for the comparison of adjectives.

Adjectives may be incorporated in the execution of nouns and verbs. Even nonmanual features may have an adjectival function, *e.g.*, *puffed cheeks, sucked in breath, etc.*

Size and shape specifiers and quantifiers for mass and count nouns provide additional descriptive adjectives for ASL.

Chapter Eight: Deafness and ASL

What is it like to be deaf?

It is not unusual for hearing people to wonder what it is like to be deaf, especially if they have personal or professional reasons for being involved with deafness and with deaf people. It is not wrong for hearing people to speculate about the experience of deafness, nor is it surprising that they might be curious or even seriously interested in knowing what it is like to be deaf. But one should not be overly optimistic that such interest or curiosity can be satisfied. The heroine in *Children of a Lesser God* refers to deafness as her secret place where no one who is hearing has ever entered. The experience of deafness is a very personal and very private experience. It cannot be pretended or imagined.

Hearing persons tend to translate the experience of deafness into their own personal reaction to becoming deaf. But to be deaf and to become deaf are not the same thing. Becoming deaf involves a loss of a sensory system on which one has come to depend for many important aspects of living. Such a loss would be a very stressful experience. One would mourn such a loss for a long time, grieving over the loss of such an important faculty. Consequently, hearing people often assume that deaf people generally feel as sad, as isolated, as frustrated, and as handicapped as they would be or feel if they suddenly lost their hearing. But this is not how deaf people perceive themselves or their condition. A deaf person is not a hearing person minus the ability to hear. One will never come to know deafness by starting with hearing. What is it like to be a deaf person? You have to be deaf to understand.

Definitions and Incidence

There is no clear definition of deafness. It may seem obvious that a deaf person is someone who cannot hear. But must deafness be total? What if a person can hear a few loud sounds? Is a very small amount of hearing sufficient to call someone hard-of-hearing rather than deaf? Or what if a person could hear up to age 70 and then experienced a severe hearing loss? Such a person may be just as deaf someone who was born deaf, but do they really have the same handicap? Clearly, the experience of deafness can differ greatly from one individual to another. Meanwhile, there are no criteria for declaring someone legally deaf.

Since there is no agreed-upon definition of deafness, it is impossible to say with certainty how many deaf people there are in the United States. As many as 16,000,000 people are believed to have some kind of hearing impairment. As many as 2,000,000 of these may have losses severe enough that they would be considered to be deaf by educators and professional workers. The Conference of Executives of American Schools for the Deaf distinguishes between a deaf person and a hard-of-hearing person on the basis of their ability to understand speech. A deaf person is someone who is unable to understand speech even with the help of a hearing aid. A hard-of-hearing person is someone who, generally with the help of a hearing aid, can understand speech. About one person in every 1,000 people in the United States is deaf according to this definition. But not all of these people were deaf from birth. If we restrict our definition of *deaf* to those whose loss is profound and occurred either from birth (congenital) or very early in life (e.g., prior to age three), the number comes closer to one deaf person for every 2,000 population members.

Degree of Loss

Audiologists classify people into categories of deafness based on their degree of loss. If we take the amount of energy required by persons with normal hearing to detect a sound as the standard for normal acuity, then, when greater intensities are required for a sound to be detected, the additional intensity can serve as an index of a hearing loss. The unit of measurement for the energy required to produce sound is a decibel (dB). If an additional 60 dB of intensity is required for a hearing-impaired person to hear a sound compared to that required by a person with normal hearing, the hearing-impaired person is reported to have a 60 dB hearing loss. It is the threshold for speech reception that is of primary interest. But speech is a complex stimulus; therefore, audiologists generally resort to an estimate based on the average threshold for pure tones at 500, 1000, and 2000 Hertz. Anything up to a 30 dB loss in this range of frequencies is considered to be a mild loss resulting in only minor inconveniences when communicating in less than ideal conditions, such as in a noisy environment or over a telephone. A 30 to 60 dB loss is a moderate loss, often requiring a hearing aid. A person with a loss within this range should still be able to hear speech well enough to understand it. A 60 to 90 dB loss is a severe loss. Even with a hearing aid speech may be hard to understand. A loss greater than 90 dB is a profound loss. A hearing aid will provide only limited benefits, such as knowing when someone is speaking, but not what is said.

Eyeglasses correct the vision of many nearsighted people. It would be wonderful if hearing aids could do the same for deaf people. But severe to profound deafness involves damage to the cochlea or auditory nerve or both. A hearing aid cannot correct such defects any more than glasses can correct for a damaged retina or optic nerve.

A hearing aid is actually of only limited benefit to a person who is profoundly deaf. One reason for this is that speech must be presented at about 30 dB above threshold to be at a comfortable listening level. If a person has a 90 dB loss, this does not leave much room for amplification.

Ninety dB plus 30 dB is 120 dB, and that is at the level of discomfort or pain for most people. Moreover, a profound hearing loss generally includes distortion of loudness or pitch or both. Many deaf people experience an increment in loudness that is greatly magnified compared to the increase in intensity that is presented. This is called *recruitment,* and it means that one cannot be sure that the same increase in physical intensity will be experienced by all deaf people as a similar increase in loudness. Moreover, deaf people are also likely to experience frequency distortions. Many deaf people retain some sensitivity to low frequency sounds but are unable to hear high frequency sounds. Since consonants are high frequency sounds, and since consonants are important for speech discrimination, even deaf people who have a fair amount of residual hearing at low frequencies may still have a great deal of difficulty understanding speech. A hearing aid can only amplify the sounds. It cannot make up for the distortion caused by greater losses in the higher frequencies. Thus, there are three factors contributing to the difficulty that deaf persons may experience with a hearing aid: (1) the limited range of intensity that is available for amplification, (2) distortion of sound intensity because of recruitment, and (3) problems with discrimination stemming from frequency distortions. Hearing aids are currently under development that would amplify sounds selectively, tailoring the output to individual losses. But even these advanced devices will not be able to eliminate all sources of distortion. The most that they will be able to do is to compensate for them to some extent.

Age at Onset and Etiology

The severity of the hearing loss is not the only variable that is important for predicting how successfully and by what means a deaf person is likely to communicate. There are two developmental milestones that are generally recognized to interact in important ways with the onset of deafness, namely, the acquisition of a spoken language and the making of a vocational choice. If deafness occurs prior to acquisition of linguistic competence (prelingual deafness), this has enormous implications for the deaf child's ability not only to learn to speak but also to learn the grammar of the spoken language. The age generally associated with linguistic competence is age three. A child whose deafness occurred prior to age three is considered to be prelingually deaf. Prelingual deafness is much more serious than postlingual deafness, not merely because the child will have more difficulty learning to make speech sounds, but also, and more importantly, because the child will not have a normal opportunity to learn the grammar of a spoken language or the rules governing its appropriate social use. Normally, children learn the grammar of a language by hearing it spoken. Even a few months of hearing may offer some benefits, and the child who became deaf at 12 or 18 months may have some advantages over a child who was born deaf. The child who is born deaf must learn by means of vision a language that was not meant to be learned that way. There are clear neurological and developmental relationships between speech and language, and the fact that spoken languages are typically learned through auditory experiences during the early years of life put the child born deaf at a clear disadvantage for learning to read or to speechread a language such as English. If a child becomes deaf after learning the basic rules of grammar, e.g., after age three, the child is said to be *postlingually* deaf. Although deafness is always a serious handicap, prelingual deafness is generally considered to be more severe than postlingual deafness because of its impact on the development of fluency in a spoken language.

The second developmental milestone associated with the consequences of deafness is vocational choice. Individuals who are prevocationally deaf tend to make a different adjustment to a hearing loss than individuals who became deaf after preparing for and entering upon a career. Career decisions made by prevocationally deaf persons will take the disability into account.

Another important distinction between deaf persons is related to etiology or the cause of deafness. Nearly half of the cases of deafness in the United States are endogenous or hereditary. Hereditary deafness may be due to a dominant gene or a recessive gene. At one time some authorities believed that one could reduce the incidence of deafness by discouraging deaf people from marrying each other, but this is no longer considered to be feasible, much less desirable. At least half the cases of hereditary deafness stem from recessive genes. Over 70 recessive genes can cause deafness. One in eight persons carries one of them. It is highly unlikely that two people will marry who have the same defective gene in the same locus. But it can happen, and one-fourth of the existing cases of deafness may be due to such a coincidence. Exogenous causes of deafness are not hereditary. They include teratogens, such as viral infections in utero, and infectious childhood diseases, such as measles or meningitis. The distinction between endogenous and exogenous causes of deafness is important because exogenous causes often cause other mental or physical defects in addition to a hearing loss. The presence of additional handicaps greatly complicates educational placement and training, and these additional handicaps also make it more difficult for the deaf individual to make a successful adjustment.

One should also distinguish between conductive hearing losses and sensorineural losses. Conductive losses occur when the ear canal is obstructed by a congenital defect, by an accumulation of wax, or by swelling caused by an infection. They also occur when the ear drum is ruptured or when the middle ear is filled with fluid from an ear infection.

A conductive loss may also occur when the bones of the middle ear are not free to move as they should, *e.g.*, from a build-up of calcium deposits. A conductive hearing loss is generally in the mild to moderate range. Since the cochlea is not defective, a bone conduction hearing aid can greatly enhance speech comprehension. Often conductive losses can be reduced or even removed entirely by medication or surgery. Sensorineural losses, on the other hand, are associated with a defective cochlea or a damaged auditory nerve or both. They cannot be cured by medicine. They are permanent. Sometimes they are progressive, that is, they continue to worsen as the individual grows older. Some progressive losses are hereditary. Many hearing losses are mixed, that is, they have both sensorineural and conductive components. A hearing aid is generally less effective for sensorineural losses than for conductive losses, because sensorineural losses usually involve some distortion in frequency or intensity.

Home and School Environments

Besides the within-subject variables of degree of loss, age of onset, etiology, and type of hearing loss, there are important environmental variables to consider, especially the variables that are associated with the home and school environments. About ten percent of deaf children have deaf parents. Most of them learn ASL from birth and participate fully as a contributing member of the family. About 90% of deaf children have hearing parents who did not anticipate that their child might have a hearing loss. It may take many months before the loss is diagnosed. The parents may have a very difficult time accepting the fact of their child's deafness and the consequences to them as a family. The parents may deny the reality of the hearing loss, seeking a miraculous cure or medical promises of relief. They are likely to mourn the loss of the healthy child that they do not have and grieve over their circumstances. Their child's deafness may become a preoccupation, standing out as the child's most important characteristic. There may be feelings of guilt over the stigma associated with a handicap in the family or over imagined wrongs for which they are being punished. It often takes a long time for parents to work through their feelings of depression, guilt, rejection, and denial. A residue may always remain a part of the experience, ready to resurface when new decisions need to be made about their child's future.

It is well established that the bond of attachment that is formed between an infant and caregiver is extremely important for the child's subsequent emotional and cognitive development. Attachment is also important for socialization, since a young child will obey the mother rather than risk rejection or separation. To the extent that deafness interferes with forming and maintaining a secure bond, deafness imposes a handicap for normal development. Fortunately for deaf children, a hearing loss does not appear to interfere with the early social interactions between the infant and caregiver. Indeed, deafness often goes undiscovered for the first year of life. But as the child grows older and does not learn to speak, one or another member of the family is likely to suspect that something is wrong. (It is amazing how frequently deafness is first identified by a grandparent.) Lack of a common language for communicating emerges as the first serious consequence of deafness. It will continue to be the most handicapping aspect of the disability. Parents typically have no prior knowledge of Sign Language and limited opportunities to discover how it might aid their communication with their deaf child. Meanwhile, the child is cut off from normal means of acquiring English. The lack of free and easy communication between parents and child is a major source of difficulty within a family whose child is deaf.

Not surprisingly, families with a handicapped child experience a considerable amount of stress, even to the point of leading to a higher incidence of divorce compared to couples whose children are not handicapped. The child with a handicap often requires a substantial investment of time and energy. Parents of a deaf child must visit doctors, audiologists, speech therapists, preschool programs, hearing aid dealers, and other specialists that parents of normal children do not have to include in their schedules. Many of these services cost additional money, and they are not likely to be fully covered by insurance. Handicaps are expensive. Parents of a handicapped child clearly need help.

Fortunately, parent programs are beginning to be organized in many communities to provide support. A good parent program should be family centered. It should take the needs of all the family members into account. A program that helps a family develop its resources for meeting the needs of all the family members will do a better job of helping the family meet the needs of the handicapped child in their midst. A parent program should provide information about deafness as the parents need it, and the information should describe deafness not only in a clinical sense but also in a social sense, explaining what it is like to be deaf and to experience life as a deaf person. Often parents are given advice and information in bits and pieces from a variety of professional workers and social agencies. The information may reflect different ideologies and conflicting biases. To prevent this, parent programs should adopt a team approach, so that the information parents receive will be integrated, and so that it can aid in planning a constructive course of action. Ideally, parents should be given an opportunity to meet deaf adults and to learn to communicate with them and with their deaf child using Sign. Foster grandparent programs have proved to be a useful means for accomplishing this. Deaf senior citizens are introduced to families with a young deaf child. By associating with elderly deaf adults, parents of deaf children are likely to discover that deafness is not as devastating an experience as they may have imagined it to be. A family-centered, team approach, which includes deaf people as part of the team, will go a long way toward helping parents with the very difficult task of parenting a deaf child.

Another variable affecting the way in which an individual adjusts to deafness is early educational experiences. Public Law 94-142 takes it for granted that preschool programs benefit handicapped children and mandates early childhood education for them. The quality of the program is extremely important. Are the staff members adequately trained in deaf education as a specialty area? Is the teacher able to communicate freely and easily with all the pupils in the classroom in whatever mode of communication is commonly used in class? Can the teacher understand the pupils when they address the teacher? Does the school staff include specialists in the areas of speech, audiology, physical education and recreation, prevocational training, personal hygiene, *etc.?* Do the facilities include the same equipment that is found in schools for normal children the same age, such as science laboratories, computers, a library, a gymnasium, an auditorium, *etc.?* Are there extracurricular activities available for the deaf children in the program, such as sports, yearbook staff, theatre, *etc.?* Are there adult deaf role models in the children's normal home and school environment? Where are the people who have completed the school's program, and what have they achieved vocationally, academically, socially? All of the variables that are associated with a deaf child's educational experience also play a role in determining the ways in which the child will adjust to life as a deaf adult.

The deaf child's home environment and educational experiences have both direct and indirect effects. They affect the child directly by providing a specific kind of linguistic environment within which the deaf child must learn to communicate with other people. The home and school environments also structure the child's opportunities to learn and to develop as a person. Equally importantly, these environmental variables influence the deaf child indirectly by affecting his or her self-esteem and his or her attitudes toward deafness, toward hearing persons, toward Sign Language, and toward oral communication. These indirect effects are difficult to measure, but there is no question that one's self esteem and one's attitudes toward learning and communicating are extremely important for one's personal and social adjustment and for all subsequent development. Therefore, when programs are designed that restructure a child's home environment or involve special educational experiences, it is not sufficient to ask whether the specific objectives of these interventions are achieved. It is also necessary to consider their effects on the larger context of the deaf child's development, including the child's self-concept, social world, and cultural values.

Two Views of Deafness

The controversy between oral and manual methods of deaf education is sometimes referred to as a *methods* war, as if the opposing positions had to do primarily with methods of communicating in the classroom. This is an oversimplification. The war is not merely between teaching methods or between methods of communicating with deaf children in school. The war is between opposing philosophies of education and between different views as to what is in the best interests of deaf adults. These two views can be characterized as a medical model, which defines deafness primarily as a physical disability, and a social/cultural model, which defines deafness primarily as an adaptation to life without hearing. The implications of these different views are far-reaching, and they lead, eventually, to a controversy over methods.

The medical model perceives deafness as a disability. The terms that are used in connection with the discovery and early response to deafness are revealing. Deafness is *diagnosed,* as if it were a disease. It is *treated,* as if it were an illness. Since it cannot be made to go away, it is fitted with a *prosthesis, e.g.,* a hearing aid, a device that may enable the disabled person to function as normally as possible in spite of the disability. The deaf client is given speech *therapy,* a word whose Greek root implies healing. Deaf people are considered to have a communication *disorder,* and they are referred to departments of speech *pathology.* Deafness imposes a *handicap,* and it is taken for granted that this handicap will create problems for normal development and for personal and social adjustment.

Since medical science cannot provide a cure for deafness, educational intervention is required. However, in school systems that follow the medical model, deafness is not accepted as a normal condition. Every effort is made to help deaf children overcome the deficit by learning to function as much like a hearing person as possible. The goal of education is to *restore* deaf people to society, implying that without such restoration, they are and would remain lost to society. Since the deaf child must learn to adjust to a hearing, speaking world, good oral communication skills are assigned first priority. Being able to communicate in a sign language is not considered to be an advantage. In fact, it may be considered a disadvantage, since it appears to be an accommodation to the handicap rather than an attempt to rise above it by learning to communicate with hearing people by means of speech and speechreading. Proponents of the medical model of deafness generally recommend that parents of deaf children refrain from using any signs or gestures except for natural gestures. The parents are urged to use speech with their children, so that the children become accustomed to oral communication from the very beginning. English is the language to be learned. Regardless how fluent deaf individuals may be in Sign, if their English skills are weak, they are given a poor prognosis for achievement in school and in society. Thus, the decision to place a high priority on oral communication skills is not made independently of other values. The perception of deafness as a disability to be overcome through educational intervention emphasizing speech and speechreading is consistent with the perception of deafness as a pathological condition which must be treated with therapy and a prosthesis.

Needless to say, this view of deafness is not shared by the large majority of deaf people in the United States. They do not tend to consider themselves a flawed people. They recognize that they have a handicap, but it surfaces mainly when they have to deal with hearing, speaking people who do not understand Sign Language or deafness. Among each other they communicate freely in ASL, enjoy the support of a personal, social network, and share a common set of values, folklore, and traditions. United by a common language and by ties of friendship that often go back to their school days, the members of the deaf community provide for each other a source of personal and social identity as well as a sense of self-worth and self-esteem. Social, athletic, religious, and alumni organizations afford many opportunities for their members to acquire leadership skills and to learn to cooperate with one another to achieve common goals. Within the deaf community deaf people enjoy the same freedom of expression and self actualization that hearing people enjoy within their circle of friends and relatives.

The main issue in the controversy can be focused on the deaf community and its role within the larger society. Is it a good thing or a bad thing? Proponents of oral education have tended to view it as a bad thing, a subculture that limits the circle of acquaintances within which deaf people can associate and, therefore, what deaf people will achieve. Proponents of the social/cultural model of deafness have tended to view it as a good thing, a source of identity, strength, and cultural values for the deaf people who belong to it. According to this latter view, if deaf people were deprived of a deaf community, they would become what sociologists call *marginal* people, unable to adjust fully and comfortably to life in the mainstream of society and lacking any reasonable alternative. Within the deaf community deafness is normal, and deaf people can participate in all of the normal activities and become a part of all of the normal relationships that characterize a human society.

A secondary issue in the controversy has to do with the status of ASL and the value of fluency in ASL as compared to English. Those who view the deaf community as a limiting subculture tend also to consider ASL to be an inferior language or not a language at all. Deaf people who are not fluent in English are termed *low verbal*, regardless how fluent they may be in ASL. This is a one-sided perspective. Members of the deaf community hold ASL in high regard and pride themselves in their ability to communicate fluently with one another. The National Association of the Deaf has issued a position paper on Communication and Language which asserts: *Inherent in our Communication Position is our recognition of American Sign Language (ASL) as a language in its own right, fully deserving of respect because of its importance to deaf people for its communication, educational, and cultural values.*

The Deaf Community

The deaf community functions on a variety of levels, local, regional, national, and international. Deaf communities tend to have their origins in the residential schools from which many of their members graduated. At these schools deaf children learned from their peers a sense of self-worth and a feeling of belonging with each other that would last for a life time. They also learned from each other a powerful, effective language, ASL, with which they could communicate freely, easily, comfortably, as if they were not handicapped at all. The ties formed among deaf peers in residential schools are so strong that the alumni organizations of residential schools for the deaf often provide the most cohesive social institution for the formation and preservation of a deaf community within a given region. The annual alumni reunion of residential schools for the deaf is typically well attended, and it gives deaf people from all over the state, even those who have moved there from elsewhere, an opportunity to renew acquaintances and to catch up on recent events.

Two examples of state-wide organizations of the deaf will serve as useful examples of the important role that such institutions play in the lives of deaf people individually and collectively. The Pennsylvania Society for the Advancement of the Deaf (P.S.A.D.) is a state-wide association many of whose members attended either the Pennsylvania School for the Deaf in Mt. Airy, PA, or the Western Pennsylvania School for the Deaf in Edgewood, PA. The P.S.A.D. has been a proving ground for deaf leadership for several decades, and it has influenced state legislation dealing with such matters as driving privileges, courtroom interpreting, insurance, civil service, and other important rights of deaf people. The Ohio School for the Deaf Alumni Association has the distinction of founding and operating Columbus Colony, a nursing home facility and home for the aged deaf in Westerville, OH. Both organizations exemplify the initiative and administrative ability of deaf people without paternalistic oversight from hearing persons.

At a local level, deaf clubs provide a meeting ground for deaf people, and religious organizations and athletic organizations sponsor events that meet a variety of deaf people's needs. Elderly deaf people derive special benefit from the personal social network that the local deaf community provides. If they fail to appear for a social function, several members of the deaf community are likely to pay a personal call to see that everything is all right. If they are hospitalized, friends and acquaintances will visit them regularly and keep them informed about important events, such as weddings, anniversaries, child births, club meetings, and other information. Although they may be cut off from physical contact with the deaf community, they continue to share in its mental life as its members keep them abreast of all the recent developments. The benefits that elderly deaf people derive from their membership with the deaf community may protect them from the "double jeopardy" that is often experienced by individuals who are discriminated against both because of age and because of their minority status in society.

Nationally the deaf community in the United States is manifest in two major organizations, the National Association of the Deaf, which represents the deaf community before political bodies in Washington, D.C., and the National Fraternal Society for the Deaf, which pioneered the offering of insurance coverage for deaf people at a time when commercial insurance companies were reluctant to accept deaf people as risks. Athletic activities are also carried out on a national scale with basketball and bowling attracting considerable interest in the United States. Soccer and volleyball are popular sports among deaf communities in Europe and South America. The National Association of the Deaf publishes a newspaper, *The Broadcaster,* and a magazine, *The Deaf American,* which keep members and other subscribers informed about issues and events of special interest to the deaf community.

At the international level the World Deaf Federation holds international meetings which provide a forum for deaf views. The Xth World Congress of the World Deaf Federation was held in 1983 in Palermo, Sicily. The XIth World Congress is scheduled for 1987 in Finland.

The International Games for the Deaf also provide an occasion for multi-national participation. The Committee of Sports for the Deaf was founded in 1924, and the first World Games for the Deaf were held in that year in Paris with athletes from nine nations participating. The II International Games were held in Amsterdam in 1928. In 1929 the Scandanavian countries, Denmark, Finland, Norway, and Sweden joined the games, and fifteen countries participated in the III International Games in Nuremberg in 1931. The United States began to participate in 1935 at the games in London. The 1985 International Games for the Deaf were held in Los Angeles with over 2500 athletes from 28 countries participating.

Deaf people who travel internationally benefit personally from the world-wide deaf community. They are always welcome in any deaf club in any city of the world.

Once one is made aware of all of the opportunities that deaf people have within the deaf community for personal development, religious and cultural experiences, athletic contests, travel, and friendships, it is hard to take seriously the suggestion that deaf people who affiliate with the deaf community and use ASL to communicate live in a restricted subculture. Deaf people who belong to the deaf community are surrounded by a personal, social network that gives meaning and purpose to their lives. Meanwhile, deaf people also live and move among hearing persons as they work, shop, vote, have neighbors, transact business, rear children, and do countless other things that are considered to be part of living in society today. Deaf people have the benefit of two cultures, the culture of the larger society in which they live and the culture of the deaf community to which they also belong.

Three New Developments

Within the past twenty-five years, three new developments have significantly improved the quality of life for deaf people in the United States. The first of these three new events is the formation of a national registry of professional interpreters for the deaf. Prior to the formation of this organization, now known as the Registry of Interpreters for the Deaf (R.I.D.), deaf people had to rely on hearing friends, neighbors, or relatives to interpret for them on the telephone or for meetings with business or professional persons. Sometimes a young hearing child had to serve as the family interpreter. The hearing people who performed these services were generally well intentioned, but they were not professionally trained, and there were no assurances that they were qualified to perform the services of an interpreter. In 1964 a conference was held at Ball State University in Muncie, Indiana, to discuss the need for professional interpreters for the deaf community. The Registry of Interpreters for the Deaf was launched at that meeting as a new professional organization. Like most professional organizations, it has gone through a period of time identifying who its members were or ought to be, what its goals were, and how it should define the services that the organization wished to offer deaf people. But it has survived as an organization, and it provides examinations and certifies members who pass these examinations as having demonstrated a specific level of proficiency in interpreting from English to ASL or *vice versa*. Many public agencies now recognize that deaf people are entitled to interpreters for the same reason that persons with a physical disability are entitled to ramps for wheel chairs. Interpreters give deaf people access to services to which U.S. citizens are entitled. Examples of situations where deaf people are entitled to an interpreter include pre- and post-operative instructions in a hospital, during child delivery, in a court of law, in a rehabilitation counseling or training situation, in public educational facilities, and other services to which the public is entitled by law. With an interpreter at their side, deaf people can participate in a broad range of activities that previously were denied them. A competent interpreter can facilitate communication between deaf and hearing people without denying the reality of the disability and without compromising deaf people's access to society.

The second important development deserving of mention is the development of telecommunication devices that make it possible for deaf people to use a telephone. Previously, deaf people could not use a telephone to check whether someone was at home before driving over for a visit. They often had to go away disappointed. There was no way they could make their own appointments with dentists, doctors, hairdressers, school teachers, *etc.* They had to ask a hearing person to make the telephone call for them. Often deaf people were denied access to jobs solely on the grounds that they could not use a telephone. Today deaf people can buy a telecommunications device that connects a keyboard to an ordinary telephone line so that messages can be transmitted between keyboards. When the destination of the call does not have a teletypewriter terminal, relay stations staffed by professionals can take the call from the deaf person and act as intermediary to complete the call. It is becoming more and more common for police departments, fire departments, hospital emergency rooms, libraries, and other public agencies to have a telecommunications device available to receive calls directly from deaf people. Some telephone companies are making concessions on rates (New York Telephone is one of them) to take into account the extra time it takes to carry on a conversation via a keyboard. Telecommunications devices have removed a major barrier separating deaf people from the rest of society.

A third major event in recent history, one that is also a technological improvement, is a provision for closed captions on televised programs. Previously, if captions were added to a program, there was no way to delete them for people who did not want them. These were open captions, and some people considered them to be distracting. Now several hours of prime time programming is closed captioned, that is, only those who wish to receive the captions do so. They must purchase a special device that attaches to the television receiver. The captions are broadcast separately over another frequency band. Having this band saved for this purpose was the first major victory for the deaf community.

Persuading broadcasters to provide captions for their programs and to transmit them over this special frequency band was the second. Now deaf people can enjoy television programming without having to guess at what is happening. The additional exposure to captioned material may contribute to their general education and fluency in English.

There have been other events, of course, of interest to the deaf community. The three above were singled out because they attack that feature of deafness that is its most important handicapping feature, namely, its barrier to easy communication with the rest of society. Interpreters, telecommunications devices, and closed captions on television give deaf people access to the rest of the world in ways that were unimaginable prior to 1960. Other events which might challenge these for significance are the following:

A large number of colleges and universities now provide educational opportunities for deaf students, including programs at the masters and doctoral levels.

Deaf persons are beginning to penetrate high level administrative positions in the field of deaf education.

A parent organization, the American Society for Deaf Children, has been established which encourages good communication between parents and their deaf children by any and all means, including Sign.

An association of professional workers with the deaf has been formed, now known as the American Deafness Rehabilitation Association, with its own professional journal, the *Journal of Rehabilitation of the Deaf.*

The Communicative Skills Program of the National Association of the Deaf has encouraged the development of classes in American Sign Language across the country in adult education programs, public schools, and colleges and universities, and it has encouraged the development of a professional organization, the Sign Instructor's Guidance Network, to establish standards for the effective teaching of ASL.

Deafpride, Inc., was launched in Washington, D.C., as an advocacy organization dedicated to bilingual education for deaf children in English and ASL and to the goal of having deaf and hearing, black and white people working together for common goals.

National and international symposia have been conducted on sign language research and teaching, and a professional journal, *Sign Language Studies,* has been published to disseminate research on Sign Languages and their use by deaf people.

The National Theatre of the Deaf was organized to present plays in spoken English and Sign and to give deaf people an opportunity for a career in the theatre; since that time deaf theatre groups have sprung up all across the country.

Cochlear implants have been developed for use with deaf adults who would not be likely to benefit from conventional hearing aids.

The important thing to note about the above achievements is that they are all recent events. Prior to 1960 it did not seem likely that individual deaf people would achieve national distinction in the fields of education, research, and public service. It would have seemed unrealistic to believe that deaf people would have available professionally trained interpreters, telecommunications devices, and closed captioned television programs to keep them in touch with the world around them. All of this has come about within the past twenty to thirty years.

What the Future May Bring

It is hazardous to be prophetic. Even the most visionary forecast of a previous era, like walking on the moon or travelling in outer space, are now history. Meanwhile, we seem to have made no progress at all in dealing with our most serious social problems. What is in store for Sign Language and for deaf people? There is little room for complacency. Except for greater tolerance for manual communication in many schools, educational methods have not changed much in the last 25 years, nor have the educational attainments of deaf youth. The public is still relatively uninformed about the nature of deafness as a handicap and about the abilities of deaf people to function as contributing members of society. Even professionals in the field of deafness are often still paternalistic, still prone to view deaf people as disabled hearing people, still inclined to think that the best thing that can be done for deaf people is to make them as much like hearing people as possible. But there are some hopeful signs. Linguists have demonstrated beyond doubt that ASL is a language. Anthropologists have provided insights into the deaf community as a normally functioning segment of the larger society. Sociologists have helped us understand that the stigma of deafness is an invention of our social order, which has not yet learned how to accept its own infirmities. Psychologists have shown that deaf children's cognitive development does not require a spoken language base and that deaf people's communicative competence in ASL reflects a normal adaptation of the visual perceptual system to their need for a shared language. If the behavioral sciences continue to inform our collective minds and conscience, there may yet be a place in our society for a group of people whom Harry Best once described as *the most misunderstood among the sons of men, but the "gamest" of them all.*

111

Supplementary Materials

Hoemann, H. W. *The American Sign Language: Lexical and grammatical notes with translation exercises.* Silver Spring, Md.: National Association of the Deaf, 1976.

Hoemann, H. W., & Hoemann, S. A. *Sign Language Flash Cards.* Vol. I. Silver Spring, MD: National Association of the Deaf, 1973.

Hoemann, H. W., Hoemann, S. A., & Lucafo, R. *Sign Language Flash Cards.* Vol. II. Silver Spring, MD: National Association of the Deaf, 1982.

Hoemann, H. W., & Lucafo, R. *I want to talk: A child model of American Sign Language.* Silver Spring, Md.: National Association of the Deaf, 1980.

Lucafo, R., & Hoemann, H. W. *Deaf models of American Sign Language: English translation.* Bowling Green, OH: WBGU-TV, 1983.

Index